W

Praise for *Five Years of My Life*

"The most compassionate, truthful, and dignified account of the disgrace of Guantanamo that you are ever likely to read."

—John le Carré

"I thank God that Murat kept his sanity in the hell of injustice and torture in Guantanamo so he could tell his story. May it be studied in every school and college around the world. May it help to close down all the illegal and secret prisons and camps, as well as Guantanamo, and restore the prisoners to their families. I am sure Murat's book will educate a whole generation about justice and the defense of human rights."

—Vanessa Redgrave

Five Years of My Life inspiringly demonstrates that, even in the face of great injustice, human dignity can shine through. Kurnaz, one of the many victims of the war on terrorism, delivers a powerful firsthand account of the abuses at Guantanamo, which should serve as a wake-up call for all those who value freedom."

—Nadine Strossen, President of the American Civil Liberties Union and Professor of Law at New York Law School

"Murat makes the horrors and inanities of Guantanamo so real; his voice is by turns young and headstrong, wry and wise. Murat's mother came to the United States to hear our first Guantanamo case argued before the Supreme Court back in 2004—when I met her, I didn't know whether she would ever see her son again. Now he is safe at home and has produced this riveting and moving account of his torture and abuse at the hands of the U.S. government to shine a light in a dark place and try to help all those still languishing without hope. This is a must read."

—Michael Ratner, President of the Center for Constitutional Rights and attorney representing the Guantánamo detainees

FIVE YEARS OF MY LIFE

An Innocent Man in Guantanamo

Murat Kurnaz

with
Helmut Kuhn

Translated by
Jefferson Chase

Foreword by
Patti Smith

palgrave
macmillan

W

FIVE YEARS OF MY LIFE
Copyright © Rowohlt Berlin Verlag GmbH, Berlin, 2007.
English-language translation copyright © 2006 by Jefferson Chase

All rights reserved. No part of this book may be used or reproduced in any
manner whatsoever without written permission except in the case of brief
quotations embodied in critical articles or reviews.

First published in Germany as *Fünf Jahre Meines Lebens* by Rowohlt Berlin

First published in English in 2008 by
PALGRAVE MACMILLAN™
175 Fifth Avenue, New York, N.Y. 10010 and
Houndmills, Basingstoke, Hampshire, England RG21 6XS.
Companies and representatives throughout the world.

PALGRAVE MACMILLAN is the global academic imprint of the Palgrave
Macmillan division of St. Martin's Press, LLC and of Palgrave Macmillan Ltd.
Macmillan® is a registered trademark in the United States, United Kingdom
and other countries. Palgrave is a registered trademark in the European
Union and other countries.

ISBN-13: 978–0–230–60374–5
ISBN-10: 0–230–60374–2

Library of Congress Cataloging-in-Publication Data

Kurnaz, Murat, 1982–
    [Fünf Jahre meines Lebens. English.]
    Five years of my life : an innocent man in Guantanamo / by Murat Kurnaz.
      p. cm.
    ISBN 0–230–60374–2
      1. Kurnaz, Murat, 1982– 2. Prisoners of war—Legal status, laws, etc.—
Cuba—Guantánamo Bay Naval Base—Biography. 3. Human rights—
Government policy—United States. 4. Combatants and noncombatants
(International law)—Biography. 5. Military bases, American—Law and
legislation—Cuba. 6. Detention of persons—Cuba—Guantánamo Bay Naval Base.
7. War and emergency powers—United States. I. Title.

KZ6496.K87 2008
973.931092—dc22
[B]   2007023633

A catalogue record for this book is available from the British Library.

Design by Newgen Imaging Systems (P) Ltd., Chennai, India.

First edition: February 2008

10 9 8 7 6 5 4 3 2 1

Printed in the United States of America.

To all the Guantanamo detainees
and their families

CONTENTS

Foreword 9
    by *Patti Smith*

Translator's Note 13

Chronology of Events 15

Map 20–21

I   Frankfurt Airport 23

II   Peshawar, Pakistan 25

III   Kandahar, Afghanistan 47

IV   Kusca, Turkey 83

V   Guantanamo Bay, Camp X-Ray 91

      Photographs 119

VI   Bremen, Hemelingen 127

VII Guantanamo Bay, Camp X-Ray 141

VIII Guantanamo Bay, Camp Delta 155

IX   Guantanamo Bay, Camp Echo 199

X   Guantanamo Bay, Camp 4 209

XI   Ramstein Air Base, Germany 221

XII Bremen, Hemelingen 229

Epilogue 239
    by *Baher Azmy*

FOREWORD

MURAT KURNAZ WAS ARRESTED IN THE WINTER OF 2001 in Peshawar, Pakistan, known as the "City of Flowers." The subsequent five years Murat spent as a detainee in the United States military prison at Guantanamo Bay Naval base, with no formal charge lodged against him, reflects a terrible flaw in our judicial system. In the case of Murat Kurnaz, the accuser had the greater power over the accused. This violation of the basic civil right to due process poses a great threat to our safety and stability as a free people.

My reaction to his ordeal is one of a mother, as well as an artist and concerned citizen. Murat Kurnaz is the same age as my own son. I could only imagine the horror and frustration his mother experienced while attempting to penetrate the labyrinth of bureaucratic secrecy that surrounded Murat's internment. I considered deeply how I would feel if my own son languished in prison, detained for years of his life without formal charge, without trial.

To compound the injustice, it was reported that most of the evidence held against Murat Kurnaz was found to be exculpatory. In truth, I had to consult my dictionary to understand the meaning of this word. I was shocked to learn it means that someone is free of guilt or blame. This information would have been a godsend to his family and council and should have enabled his quick release. Instead, Murat languished in prison for another four years, even after it became clear to both U.S. and foreign authorities that he was innocent.

In the summer of 2006, after exhaustive negotiations on his behalf, Murat reclaimed his freedom. This long-awaited moment, his release after nearly five years of harsh detention, turned instead into a shocking continuation of his confinement. Muzzled and shackled for the duration of a seventeen-hour flight, Murat was returned to his homeland in the same manner one might transport a dangerous animal. The image of this young man, who had already experienced years of deprivation and humiliation, limping in chains drew from within me a deep sense of outrage.

Yet this final dehumanizing act did not break Murat Kurnaz. He found the strength to meditate on these events in his memoir, to reclaim his individuality, to openly practice his faith, to once again ride a motorbike and listen to music. Though the crown of his youth was taken from him, he offers us his experiences unfettered by the poison of bitterness.

When in prison Murat Kurnaz prayed for patience and strength. Surely the Most Excellent Protector shepherded him through his suffering, and the qualities that he prayed for will continue to illuminate his life.

PATTI SMITH

Without Chains

four long years
was I a man
dreaming in chains
with the lights on
a netherworld
nothing to say
thoughts impure
at Guantanamo Bay

now I'm learning
to walk
without chains
I'm learning
to walk
without chains
without chains
without chains

born in Bremen
played guitar
a young apprentice
building ships
loved and married
heard the call
is attaining wisdom
a pursuit of fools?

journeyed to Pakistan
to study Koran
taken in custody
no reason why
then a prison camp
no freedom to breathe

branded an enemy
an enemy

(Chorus)

no fault was found
yet do they believe
then flown home
a version of free
chained to the floor
muzzled and bound
a last humiliation
left to endure
they say I walk
strange
that may be so
its been a long time
since I walked at all

now I'm learning
to walk
without chains
to talk
without chains
to breathe
without chains
to pray
without chains
to live
without chains
without chains

Patti Smith
copyright 2007

TRANSLATOR'S NOTE

DESPITE BEING BORN IN GERMANY AND HAVING LIVED his whole life there, Murat Kurnaz was not a German citizen at time of his detention in Guantanamo. German citizenship law is based primarily on ethnicity and family relation. Thus, the descendents of the numerous Turkish immigrants who worked to help rebuild postwar Germany, though born in the country, are not automatically issued German passports. Since obtaining German citizenship is a complicated process—and residence permits entitle holders to most of the rights afforded by the state to citizens—many "foreigners" in Germany simply opt to live as permanent resident aliens.

Kurnaz wrote this account of his years in Guantanamo in conjunction with a German journalist named Helmut Kuhn, who helped him shape his story into a narrative. I have chosen to omit some typical German narrative techniques—chiefly transitions from the narrative past to the present tense to build tension—from this translation. These techniques are unfamiliar in English and would, I felt, only have created confusion.

The issue of how to translate the Koran is highly contentious, as there is no standard English rendering of the book. I have tried to convey the sense of the Koranic quotations and other religious material in this book as neutrally as possible and would ask for readers' indulgence of any infelicities.

JEFFERSON CHASE
May 2007

CHRONOLOGY OF EVENTS

OCTOBER 3, 2001: A few weeks after the September 11 attacks on the United States, 19-year-old Murat Kurnaz flies to Karachi, Pakistan, without telling his parents he is leaving. He spends some eight weeks traveling the country and visiting various mosques.

OCTOBER 7, 2001: The U.S.-led war in Afghanistan begins.

OCTOBER 11, 2001: Prosecutors in Bremen begin investigating Kurnaz and three others "on suspicions of their having formed a criminal organization." The investigations come after Kurnaz's mother tells police that her missing son had changed recently, growing a beard and becoming religious. One of Kurnaz's teachers at his shipbuilding school cites unnamed students as reporting that Kurnaz was going to Afghanistan.

DECEMBER 1, 2001: On the way to the airport in Peshawar, Kurnaz is stopped at a police checkpoint. He spends several days in Pakistani jails before being handed over to the U.S. military, who take him to a U.S. military base in Kandahar, Afghanistan.

JANUARY 9, 2002: The German Intelligence Agency informs the German government under Chancellor Gerhard Schröder that Kurnaz—a Turkish citizen who was born and raised in Germany—is being held in Kandahar.

JANUARY 11, 2002: The first prisoners are brought from Afghanistan to the U.S. military base in Guantanamo Bay, Cuba.

FEBRUARY 1, 2002: Kurnaz's mother writes to the German Foreign Office asking for help in obtaining information about her son. Police inform her that he is to be transferred to Guantanamo.

FEBRUARY 2, 2002: Kurnaz is flown to Guantanamo.

FEBRUARY 15, 2002: The German Federal Prosecutor's Office refuses to take over the investigations concerning Kurnaz from local Bremen prosecutors, citing the lack of "clear evidence" indicating "the formation of a terrorist association."

FEBRUARY 20, 2002: Investigators from the Office for the Protection of the Constitution in Bremen interview Kurnaz's fellow students, including some openly hostile to him. A note from those interviews records "no direct statements that [Kurnaz] wanted to fight against the Americans in Afghanistan."

APRIL 28, 2002: Together with some three hundred other Guantanamo prisoners, Kurnaz is transferred from Camp X-Ray to the newly built Camp Delta.

MAY 27, 2002: German attorney Bernhard Docke begins representing Murat Kurnaz.

SEPTEMBER 23–24, 2002: Two officials from the German Intelligence Agency travel to Guantanamo and interrogate Kurnaz for twelve hours under CIA supervision. After the interrogations, one of the officials notes that "in the estimation of our U.S. allies a considerable number of the detainees are not part of the terrorist milieu." His colleague, however, notes: "Against the backdrop of Kurnaz's possibly imminent release, the question must be addressed as to whether the return of this Turkish citizen is in Germany's interest, or whether, in light of the expected media attention, everything possible should be done to prevent his return."

SEPTEMBER 26, 2002: The German Intelligence Agency informs the government in Berlin by cable that "the U.S. sees Murat Kurnaz's innocence as established" and that he will be released in six to eight weeks.

OCTOBER 13, 2002: Bremen authorities suspend their investigations of Kurnaz.

OCTOBER 27, 2002: Three Afghans and a Pakistani become the first inmates released from Guantanamo. They reveal to the international media that they had been physically abused and held in solitary confinement.

NOVEMBER 8, 2002: After weeks of deliberations, the Federal Office for the Protection of the Constitution tells the CIA that, should Kurnaz be released, it is their "express wish" that he not be returned to Germany.

MARCH 19, 2003: The U.S.-led war in Iraq begins.

NOVEMBER 19, 2003: German Foreign Minister Joschka Fischer raises Kurnaz's case with Secretary of State Colin Powell, but no agreement is reached.

MAY 12, 2004: The city of Bremen declares that Kurnaz's German residency permit officially expired in May 2002. This decision would later be overturned by a Bremen court.

JUNE 28, 2004: The U.S. Supreme Court rules that prisoners in Guantanamo have a right to challenge their incarceration via the American legal system.

JULY 2, 2004: Kurnaz's mother petitions a U.S. court for her son's release on the grounds that it violates the U.S. Constitution, the Geneva Convention, and international law concerning human rights. Similar petitions are filed on behalf of sixty-three other prisoners.

SEPTEMBER 30, 2004: Murat Kurnaz appears before a Combatant Status Review Tribunal in Guantanamo. He—together with all the other prisoners who appear before such tribunals—is classified as an "enemy combatant."

OCTOBER 8, 2004: U.S. attorney Baher Azmy visits Kurnaz in Guantanamo for the first time.

JANUARY 31, 2005: Senior U.S. District Court Judge Joyce Hens Green rules that some of the conditions and treatment of the prisoners in Guantanamo, including the trials conducted by the military tribunals, violate the U.S. Constitution. She specifically addresses the case of Kurnaz, citing the fact that, in the estimation of German authorities, there is no hard evidence connecting him with terrorist activities.

NOVEMBER 22, 2005: Angela Merkel succeeds Gerhard Schröder as German Chancellor.

NOVEMBER 30, 2005: A Bremen court reverses the decision concerning the expiration of Kurnaz's residence permit.

DECEMBER 19, 2005: Kurnaz's German attorney, Bernhard Docke, writes to Chancellor Merkel, reminding her of his client, who he says "has been held in Guantanamo for four years in inhumane conditions."

JANUARY 13, 2006: Merkel raises the issue of Kurnaz with President George W. Bush during an official visit to Washington.

JANUARY 17, 2006: The German Chancellor's Office decides that Germany will readmit Kurnaz to the country, should he be released.

JUNE 29, 2006: The U.S. Supreme Court rules by a 5–3 margin that the military tribunals in Guantanamo are unconstitutional.

JULY 13, 2006: At a meeting in the German city of Stralsund, Merkel and Bush once again discuss Kurnaz. The U.S. and German governments are actively engaged in negotiations concerning his release.

AUGUST 24, 2006: Kurnaz is released and flown to the U.S. Air Base in Ramstein, Germany. He remains under the surveillance of the Office for the Protection of the Constitution until December 2006.

NOVEMBER 22, 2006: Kurnaz testifies before of the European Union Parliament's Special Investigations Committee Concerning the CIA.

JANUARY 17–18, 2007: Kurnaz testifies in front of a special investigations committee of the German Bundestag, established to determine whether he was physically abused by German soldiers while being held at the U.S. military base in Kandahar.

JANUARY 23, 2007: The EU Parliament's Special Investigations Committee Concerning the CIA releases its final report, which includes Kurnaz's descriptions of being tortured. The report states: "As early as 2002 the intelligence agencies of the U.S. and Germany concluded that Murat Kurnaz had no connections to either Al Qaeda or the Taliban, and did not represent a terrorist threat."

FIVE YEARS
OF
MY LIFE

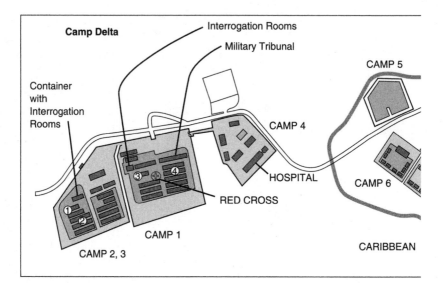

Camp Delta

Interrogation Rooms

Military Tribunal

Container with Interrogation Rooms

CAMP 5

CAMP 4

HOSPITAL

RED CROSS

CAMP 6

CAMP 1

CAMP 2, 3

CARIBBEAN

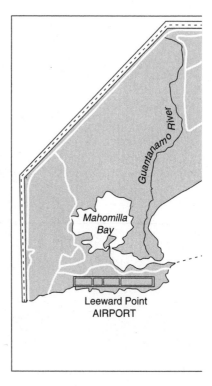

Guantanamo River

Mahomilla Bay

Leeward Point
AIRPORT

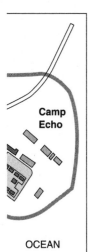

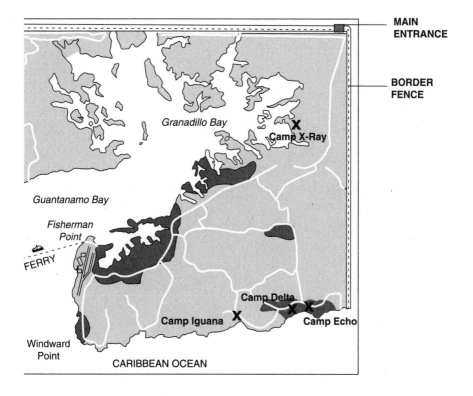

1 Block Tango
2 Block Romeo and Québec
3 Block India
4 Block Delta

Camp
Echo

OCEAN

MAIN
ENTRANCE

BORDER
FENCE

Granadillo Bay

X
Camp X-Ray

Guantanamo Bay

Fisherman
Point

FERRY

Camp Delta
X X
Camp Iguana X
Camp Echo

Windward
Point

CARIBBEAN OCEAN

I

FRANKFURT AIRPORT

I F I HAD TOLD MY MOTHER THAT I INTENDED TO TRAVEL TO Pakistan, she wouldn't have let me go. Even though I was nineteen years old, she would have forbidden me to get on the plane.

The problem was how to say good-bye to her without making it look like that was what I was doing. I decided to tell her my back was hurting and ask her for a massage. I could hug her in thanks afterward. That would be my good-bye.

I went upstairs, saying: "Ana, my back hurts. Can you give me a massage?"

"It's very late," my mother said. "I'll give you one tomorrow."

I stood on the stairs. My mother was in her bedroom. I couldn't see her in the darkness.

"Salam alaikum," I said.

"Alaikum salam," she answered.

I wouldn't see my mother again until I was twenty-five.

My bags were packed, and I had my passport, my visa, and my plane tickets. My friend Selcuk would be waiting for me in the car. My plane was scheduled to take off from Frankfurt Airport around noon.

I also wanted to say good-bye to my brothers, but I couldn't just give them a hug. Ali always wanted me to lie down next to him in bed while he was trying to fall sleep. He'd ask me questions until his eyelids started to droop. So the night before I left, I said: "Ali, I'll come to your room. Let's talk for a while." That made him happy. After a while, just before he fell asleep, I said that I was going to my room for a minute. I gave him and my baby brother Alper a kiss and then turned off the light.

At the airport I felt uneasy. I wanted to tell my mother that I would be back and that she shouldn't worry about me. At 10 AM, I called her from a pay phone.

"Where are you?" she asked.

She had already discovered that I'd packed my things and left.

"I'm in another city . . . not in Bremen. I'm going away for a little while, but I'll be back soon. Don't worry . . ."

She started crying.

"Where are you going? Come back here immediately," she said.

"I'm just going traveling for a couple of weeks. Don't cry."

She didn't stop crying, but I had to hang up because I didn't want to miss my plane. There was no way I could tell her that I was flying to Pakistan.

She wouldn't have let me go.

And that would have been a good thing.

II

PESHAWAR, PAKISTAN

'LL NEVER FORGET THE DATE: DECEMBER 1, 2001. THAT WAS when I was supposed to fly from Peshawar back to Germany. My friend Mohammad had helped me pack my gifts, and I had said good-bye to other *tablighis*, or Muslim pilgrims, at the mosque. Then we boarded the bus to Peshawar airport.

"Are you looking forward to getting home?" Mohammad asked me. "Tomorrow you'll be seeing your mother."

───────────

I had a second piece of luggage with me, a backpack with my personal belongings, as well as a belt in which I kept my money and papers. Mohammad was carrying my bag. I was originally supposed to fly back to Germany from Karachi, and Mohammad was accompanying me to the airport to help change my flight so I could depart from Peshawar. I couldn't wait to get back to Bremen. My wife was scheduled to arrive there before the end of the year from Turkey.

For the first time since I had arrived in Pakistan, I was wearing my shiny black Hugo Boss overcoat. It had remained in my backpack for the entire trip because it was much too warm. I'd thought the fall weather in Pakistan would be the same as it is in Germany and had brought heavy pants and sweaters with me from Bremen. I wanted to look stylish in Koran school and on the street.

When I arrived in Karachi on October 3 in my wool sweater and over-coat, I'd discovered that autumn in Pakistan was as warm as summer in Bremen. So most of the time I just wore T-shirts and my KangaROOS-brand hiking boots. A year later in Guantanamo, a representative of the German government would accuse me of walking around Pakistan in combat boots.

I had bought some sweets for my parents. The packages were lovely, like little works of art—it would have been a shame to eat them. For my baby brother, Alper, I had bought a handmade wooden toy, a game, with rings on a tree with braches. For myself, I had bought a pair of motorcy-cle gloves made of quality leather that would have cost a couple hundred marks in Bremen. I also had a handmade necklace for my mother, made of wood, leather, and blue lapis lazuli.

The bus we took to the airport was painted in bright colors and dec-orated with ornamental figurines. There were little bells and strings of red and yellow blinking party lights—it looked like a disco. All the buses in Pakistan look like this. The one I was traveling in was a small vehicle with a sliding door with maybe ten people in it—there was no room for anyone else. Two men had sat next to Mohammad so I had to take a seat in the row behind him.

We came to a checkpoint. I had already been through four or five such checkpoints while traveling from mosque to mosque with Mohammad and the other *tablighis*—there are checkpoints all over Pakistan. They're part of normal everyday life.

Checkpoints are usually located at police stations and are manned by one or two officers. The police attach a cord or rope to a house or a pole on the other side of the street and an officer sits in a chair sipping tea.

Whenever he wants someone to stop, he'll pull the rope taut, and the approaching cars have to brake. If he doesn't feel like checking anyone, he just leaves the rope lying slack on street and everyone drives over it. Sometimes he'll pull up the rope and take a quick glance through the windows of a vehicle before waving it on. I had never been checked personally.

On the day I was set to leave Pakistan, the policeman at the checkpoint pulled the rope. The little bells in the bus jingled as the bus came to a halt. Traffic piled up behind us. The policeman got up from his chair and peered through the window, noticing me. I looked different than the other passengers—I have fairer skin, and that's probably what attracted his attention. He knocked on the window and said something to me in Urdu. Mohammad opened the window and answered for me. I have no idea what he said to the policeman.

Then the policeman addressed me again. I told him in German that I couldn't understand because I didn't speak his language.

Of course, he didn't know what I was saying either. He asked me for my papers—at least I think he did. I got them out of my belt and handed them over. Then he said something else and motioned for me to get out of the bus. I took my backpack, squeezed my way through the other passengers, and got off. Behind us, in the line of cars, people were honking their horns.

Mohammad tried to get out with me, but it took him a while to get to the door because the bus was packed with passengers holding luggage on their laps. The policeman motioned for the bus driver to move to the side of the road. The bus driver closed the door. Mohammad was still inside.

I never saw him again.

I had met Mohammad a couple of weeks earlier in Islamabad where I was hoping to join a group of *tablighis*. *Tablighis* are students of the Koran who travel from mosque to mosque, praying and studying the holy book. I only knew a few words of English at the time. Mohammad was several years older than me and spoke English quite well since he was Pakistani, and Pakistan used to be a British colony. He also spoke some Turkish so he could translate and explain things to me. We traveled together until I was arrested that day in Peshawar.

The name Peshawar is Indian in origin, Mohammad told me, and means "city of flowers." I found that fascinating. Peshawar is a very old city, and Mohammad told me that many major historical figures, including Alexander the Great, had visited it. Muslim Arabs and Turks went to Pakistan a thousand years ago and brought Allah's revelations with them.

When he introduced me to the imams at the mosques we visited, Mohammad always said with pride: Murat is German, but he's also Turkish, like our forefathers. The Pashtun tribesmen, who introduced Islam to what is now Pakistan, are thought to originally come from Turkey. It was they who cultivated Pakistan, building gardens and parks with palm trees and flowers.

The last mosque we stayed at with the other *tablighis* was one of the largest in Peshawar. It was so big that all the mosques in Bremen could fit inside it. The rooms for Koran students were located on a spacious interior courtyard, and there, too, flowers were everywhere. The minarets stretched toward the sky. When I knelt on the rugs in the prayer halls, I felt almost intoxicated by the decorations on the walls and under the domed ceiling. Mohammad told me that a century ago there had been a huge fire in the bazaars in front of the mosque but the mosque itself had been spared from any damage because the faithful had congregated there and prayed. Mohammad said Allah had protected them.

In the weeks before we arrived in Peshawar, we had visited a number of mosques in Islamabad. Every day we studied the Koran. We were taught how to read and interpret the Koran and how to pray. We were also given hadith instruction—the Prophet Mohammed's oral teachings. We learned how we were supposed to behave as *tablighis* and how we could help other people. Twice daily, we had meals together. We went shopping and argued about who would get the honor of paying.

We would sleep in one mosque and then spend the whole of the next day in the other mosques, visiting the other *tablighis* and drinking tea with them.

The streets and bazaars of Peshawar are crowded, sticky, and hot. They stink of exhaust fumes and rotting garbage. Taxi drivers constantly honk their horns along with the drivers of the motorcycle rickshaws, which look like miniature three-wheeled trucks with a single headlight. The roads are always jam-packed with cars, horses, donkeys, completely overloaded trucks, pedestrians, and bicycles, which are sometimes used to transport large objects like refrigerators or sofas. The people on the streets come from everywhere, from India and Afghanistan, China and Kashmir.

Some of the streets have marked lanes, but everyone ignores them—it's every man for himself. As taxis, mopeds, and rickshaws push their way through the crowds, you have to be quick on your feet to avoid getting run over.

The day before I was scheduled to leave, I walked through the bazaars to buy some gifts to take back home. The bazaars in Pakistan reminded me of the open-air markets in Germany and of Oktoberfest, only much more colorful and wild. There are gold- and silversmiths, spice dealers and butchers, rug merchants and potters. There are shops with electronics, cell phones, and cameras. You can buy fake Nike sneakers, Rolex watches, and Fila jackets. The merchants sell anything and everything a person might need. There are also storytellers and shows with exotic animals and snakes. I had never seen anything like it, even on television. A snake charmer laid rope out in a circle and then sat in the middle. He removed the lids of the baskets around him, and various kinds of snakes slithered out—cobras, vipers, and other highly poisonous reptiles. The charmer closed his eyes and touched the snakes, tapping on their heads. He didn't hurt them; he was just playing with them. All of this took place in the middle of the street for free. People gave him money only if they felt like it.

I was particularly fascinated by the martial arts shows at the Kung Fu schools. Pakistan borders China, so there are many good martial arts coaches there and Kung Fu and ninja schools abound. Mohammad and I often went to watch ninjas throwing Chinese stars and knives and show-fighting. There are no laws against this kind of show in Pakistan—you can live the way you want. I found I liked this kind of freedom.

That is, until the day I took the bus to the airport.

I was told to go inside the police station with the officer. He nodded twice and pointed to the entrance of the building, which had no door.

Okay, I thought, they want to check my visa and my passport. Mohammad would wait for me, and as soon as this was over, I could continue on my way.

The station was a squat structure, and I entered a room with rugs on the floor as in a mosque. There were no furnishings. A naked light bulb hung from the ceiling. There was no desk, just a small wooden table for drinking tea in the corner. The policeman tried to tell me something, but it didn't work. We couldn't understand each other. From his gestures, I gathered that he was leaving, but that he would be right back.

A short time later, another officer appeared, probably the first one's boss. He was of medium height and slightly overweight. He had a huge moustache and a five o'clock shadow. He was wearing a turban and traditional Pakistani dress, a knee-length cotton tunic with white cotton pants. He said something to me in English. I think he was asking me where I came from. I said was from Germany. Then he wanted to know if I was a journalist.

"No," I said.

Was I an American?

"No."

Was I working for the Americans?

I told him I was a Turkish citizen who lived in Germany.

He asked whether I worked for Germany. Or for the Germans—I couldn't really tell.

The man with the turban was holding my Turkish passport in his hands. He didn't seem to understand how I could be both German and Turkish, how Germany could be my home country even though I didn't have a German passport. He probably thought he had caught me out in a lie. Maybe he thought I was a spy or something.

"Do you have cameras?" he asked.

I tried to tell him that he was welcome to look through my things and held out my backpack. "Look! Look!"

They went through my backpack. The man with the turban said something to the other officer, who then fetched a telephone from one of the other rooms in the building. It was a regular landline phone with a cord. The boss called someone—I assumed he was talking about me with his superiors. Then he hung up and said something to the other officer. He took the telephone away and reappeared with a key, a tiny mirror, a razor, and some shaving cream.

His boss shaved.

Like the entrance to the building, the room had no doors. While the head policeman was calmly shaving his face, I could hear a loud exchange of words outside. I was sure it was Mohammad, trying to get in to see me. But I could only make out the voice of the first officer.

I was standing in the middle of the room with my backpack on the floor in front of me. The first officer came and went as his boss ordered him to bring him one thing or another. One time it was a submachine gun.

Other policemen, also carrying machine guns, came into the room. They grabbed me and led me away, but not back to the street, where I thought Mohammad would be waiting. Instead I was taken to a courtyard where a four-door pick-up truck was waiting. The driver and one of the policemen got in up front, and I got into the backseat flanked by two other officers with machine guns. Another two policemen climbed onto the tailgate.

We drove through the city for maybe half an hour until we reached an affluent-looking part of town, full of large villas with big gardens and tall gateways. We drove through one of the gates, across a kind of park and through a second gateway, behind which there were a lot of fruit trees. It looked like private property, but there were guards at every entrance. We stopped and a man with blond hair and glasses approached the truck.

I couldn't tell whether he was American or German. For all I know he could have been Russian, but he was wearing European clothing, a white shirt and black pants, which isn't all that common in Pakistan.

The two-story villa had orange trees in front, a real Turkish garden. I estimated the blond man to be between thirty-five and forty years old, although he was already losing his hair. He rubbed his hands together, as if pleased about something, and spoke to the policemen in a language I didn't understand. He told me in English to come with him. The policemen followed us. He led me into a room that reminded me of a four-star hotel. It had a double bed, a framed mirror, carpets and large plants.

He disappeared for a short time and then returned with another man who looked Pakistani and wore civilian clothing. They began questioning me.

Was I American?

Was I German?

Was I a journalist?

I tried as best as I could to explain that I wanted to catch a plane back to Germany, that I didn't have much time if I failed to make a flight today. That I had missed the date on my return ticket, November 4, but that it was still valid for another flight for ninety days.

The men said they would come back and ask me some more questions. I was to wait there.

I waited for about an hour.

The two men in civilian clothing never returned. Instead the policemen came back.

———————————

Should I have tried to flee while I was alone in that room? The doors in the villa weren't locked. But where could I have gone? Guards and policemen were everywhere with machine guns. I thought there was probably just a problem with my visa. I hadn't done anything wrong in Pakistan—I hadn't stolen anything or hurt anyone. I was sure that they weren't going to detain me for more than a couple of hours. They just wanted to ask me a few questions—that was all. I wasn't worried. I was merely irritated that they were taking so much time.

I didn't think that being stopped at the checkpoint might be connected with the war in Afghanistan. I had nothing to do with that country although it did occur to me that maybe they thought I was a drug dealer. Afghanistan is one of the world's biggest opium suppliers. But I wasn't carrying any drugs, and I hadn't had contact with any dealers. As soon as they found out I wasn't a dealer, a journalist, or an American, I thought, I'd be set free.

The officers drove me in the pick-up to a police station near the villa. They told me I was going to have to spend the night there. The following morning I would be taken to the airport and I could fly to Turkey. Why Turkey? I asked. I was from Germany! Then it occurred to me that Mohammad still had my bag. The bag with my gifts. I hoped that he would be at the airport the next day and could somehow help me to get back to Germany.

We arrived at the police station. It looked exactly like the first one: the entrance didn't have a door, and the first room I saw was carpeted. I hadn't been handcuffed. The place didn't feel like a prison.

"You sleep here," said one of the policemen in English. "Tomorrow we come, bring you to airport. You Turkish, you fly to Turkey."

I thought he meant that I was to sleep on one of the carpets, but I was wrong. They opened a door, behind which I saw bars. This was a jailhouse after all.

The policemen led me through the door, opened the single, large cell and pushed me in. The cell was fifteen by thirty square feet, and it was full of people, all of them dark-skinned men, most likely Pakistanis or Afghans. There were around fifty of us crowded in there. They looked me over and then greeted me. They were friendly. Suddenly everyone stepped aside and formed an aisle. A young man in his thirties came up to me. He seemed to be the boss of the cell. He greeted me.

"Salam alaikum."

"Alaikum salam."

The man's name was Raheg, and he shook my hand. "Do you want to be my guest?" he asked in English. "Will you come with me, please?"

Raheg led me through a door at the back of the cell into a separate room—his own private prison cell. It was comfortable. He had a bed, a pillow, and a low table with a tea pot, glass tea cups and some cheese on a silver platter.

Raheg was powerfully built and much bigger than me. He must have been at least 6′3″ and 250 pounds. In contrast to the other prisoners, he seemed like a rich man. He might have been incarcerated with the rest of us, but when he told the policeman to go and fetch something for him, they went and got it—pizza, hot dogs, whatever he desired. He asked me what I wanted.

Nothing, I said.

People visited him the whole afternoon. Every time the policemen would unlock the door, it was almost as though they were announcing visitors to a lord. They seemed to be afraid of him. Raheg was apparently not just the boss of the cell, but the boss of the whole jailhouse. He had gas tanks and a stove in his room. It was Ramadan at the time, and I was fasting during the day. He fasted, too. In the evening, he rolled out his prayer rug and invited me to pray with him. He gave me a brand-new shirt. My shirt was covered with dust—in Pakistan you have to change shirts every day because of the heat. Raheg told me he'd have my shirt washed. I took a shower in the main cell and changed my clothes, and then dinner was ready. The other prisoners had cooked it. There was meat, potatoes, and rice—even a salad. We talked almost the whole night through.

He told me that he had once been a major drug dealer. It was a family tradition—his forefathers had traded opium, and all his relatives were involved in the business. He had smuggled in large quantities from Afghanistan over the Khyber Pass, and now he couldn't get out of jail. He had fresh fruit brought to him and made some mint tea. He told me not to say a single word to the police. Whoever I was and whatever I'd done, I should under no circumstances tell them anything. I said I'd already told them everything.

"From now on, no more," he said. "You don't say anything. That's better for you."

Okay, I thought, he's been in prison for a number of years. He should know what's right and what's wrong here.

Raheg told me about his family, Pashtuns, some of whom lived in Afghanistan and some in Pakistan. Among Pashtuns, it's a rule that whenever someone seeks refuge in your home, for whatever reason, you should provide them protection, accommodation, and assistance. I knew from Mohammad that this tradition was like a law. Raheg said he would talk to the policemen and try to secure my freedom. He gave me several telephone numbers—of his brothers and other relatives. I could call them when I got out, he said, and they would take care of me. He told me not to worry about money. They would give me some.

"No problem," he said. "You can fly to Germany."

Pashtuns have their own rules. Raheg was good to me.

The following day, we prisoners all prayed together. Then the guards came. They were carrying chains and were going to shackle me, but Raheg flew into a rage. He came up to them, screaming. The other prisoners stood behind him. It looked as though the situation was about to escalate, but then the guards withdrew. After a while, they reappeared without the chains. I took my leave of Raheg, giving him a hug. The guards led me away. A car—a limousine with tinted windows—was waiting outside. Two policemen were sitting there, carrying machine guns.

After we had turned the first corner, we stopped. One of the policemen got out and retrieved the chains from the truck of the vehicle. They bound me, and we drove on. The policeman apologized to me with a word I recognized from Turkish.

"*Mecburi*," he said. That means: I have no choice—it's my duty.

We drove for several hours before stopping in front of a building. I couldn't tell whether it was a prison. One of the policemen got out and started talking with someone, who got excited and raised his voice. I saw kids on bicycles. They came up to the car and peered through the windows, pointing their fingers at me and laughing.

"Osama, Osama!" they cried.

When the policeman got back to the car, he was carrying a sack. He slipped it over my head. Everything went dark.

We drove for hours—at least that's how it seemed to me. It was so hot in the limousine that I thought I was going to suffocate. I tried to make this clear to the policeman sitting next to me. He lifted the sack a bit so I could breathe more easily, but the other officer yelled at him. From time to time, he lifted the sack a bit so I could get some air.

We stopped.

The policemen led me up some stairs, and I could hear a number of doors closing behind me. We went down a long corridor. Our footsteps echoed. Then I heard another door closing. From the sound, it had to be made of metal.

"Stop!"

They removed the sack from my head. I was standing in the middle of an empty room. There was no sink, no toilet, nothing other than brick walls. Behind the metal door that I had heard was another one made of heavy wood. The floor was concrete. High up one of the walls, directly under the ceiling, was a deep round hole that allowed light into the room. They took off the chains. Then they closed the door behind them. I still thought that they would come, ask me some questions, and then take me to the airport.

Hours later, I heard footsteps. A man in civilian clothes, a long shirt, vest and turban, came and asked me questions in English.

Who are you? What's your name? How old are you?

Where do you come from?

Are you a journalist?

Are you German?

Turkish?

Why did you come here?

What did you do in Pakistan?

Are you married?

Are you married to a Pakistani woman?

The questioning went on for hours. The man's English was hardly any better than mine. I told him about the *tablighis* and about Mohammad. Repeatedly, I asked him if I could use a telephone.

Finally he agreed to bring me a phone. "No problem," he said. He left the room and shut the door behind him.

I never saw that man again.

I tried to count the number of days, but I could only guess. I didn't know whether it was night or day. The light was always on. Whenever I thought it was night because I was tired, I'd try to sleep. When I thought it was daytime, I'd get up and say my morning prayers. They had taken my watch, my belt, and my shoes. I was barefoot. The only things I had in my possession were the pants I'd been wearing the whole time and the shirt Raheg had given me.

Two guards watched over me. It seemed to me that they worked in shifts of twelve hours each. But their comings and goings were irregular. Sometimes, one would appear a number of times in a row, and then the other. Sometimes, suddenly, there was no one there at all. I was able to talk with one of them a bit. The other remained silent the entire time.

They brought me food. Red lentils. Always red lentils that had been boiled but were no longer warm. Half a glass of red lentils per day. And a glass of water twice a day—at least I think it was twice a day. The times varied. Sometimes I imagined they were skipping the odd meal. I always had to ask for water by kicking the wooden door.

I also had to kick the door with my bare feet when I needed to go to the toilet. Outside there was another, equally bare room with a "squat toilet"—a hole in the floor that can be flushed. Further on there was a second metal door behind which the guards sat. Sometimes I had to kick the wooden door for hours, before one of the guards would open up and let me go to the bathroom. I refused to use the floor of my cell. I had no choice but to hold out for as long as it took.

I had to hold out.

At some point during my confinement, I became afraid. What would happen if my plane ticket expired? I didn't have any money to buy a replacement. Would they buy me one? Even if it was only a ticket to Turkey, anywhere was better than here.

I kicked the wooden door and paced across the floor of my cell.

The cell was six by nine feet. I paced back and forth. Life can't go on like this, I thought. I'll go crazy. Back and forth. I had read once that people can go insane if they spend too much time in solitary confinement. Back and forth. I needed something to occupy my mind. I went back to the door and kicked it with my bare feet. I had to do something to keep my wits.

I heard steps and the sound of a key turning.

It was the guard who talked.

I asked him if I could have a Koran. "Koran, Koran," I said. "Can I have?"

"Yes, yes."

He nodded, smiling, and shut the door. The sound of his footsteps receded, and I heard the second metal door closing. I waited, pacing around my cell. For hours and hours.

As best as I can guess, it was two days before the guard brought me a Koran.

"Koran," he said, as he handed me the book.

"Elhamdulillah," I said.

Thanks and all praise be to Allah.

The guard immediately left, and I stood holding the book in my hands. It was a beautiful moment. I opened the book and read: "In the name of God, the Mercy-giving, the Merciful! Praise be to God, Who created Heaven and Earth and granted darkness and light! Yet those who disbelieve make other things equal to their Lord. He is the One Who has created you (all) from clay; then fixed a term. A deadline [for the Day of Judgment] has been set by Him."

The sixth sura. I could hardly believe I was hearing the words of the Koran. I listened to my own voice as I read the verses. I was a prisoner, but at least I had something to do, something worthwhile even. I could study the Koran. I knew that this would be a good deed earned to my credit.

"He is God in (both) Heaven and Earth. He knows your secrets and anything you publish; He knows whatever you earn."

Suddenly I heard footsteps and keys. The door opened.

Pakistani policemen in turbans and uniforms came in and took the Koran away from me. They were carrying chains, heavy, rusty iron chains. The cuffs they clamped around my wrists were as thick as bars of chocolate. Using an Allen key, they attached the chains with screws to the inside of the handcuffs, tightening them until pain shot through my wrists. They used the same procedure with my feet. There was a further chain attached to the handcuffs with which they could lead me. I knew what was coming next.

One of them slipped the potato sack over my head.

It went dark again.

The chains rattled as they led me from the cell. I heard the wooden door and the metal door close behind it. They pulled me through the empty room with the toilet, the second metal door, the room where the guards waited, and then another metal door and a long corridor. I heard door after door closing behind me. Then I sensed light. It was daytime. I was sitting in a car, policemen to my left and right.

The sun did me some good, although I could only feel and not actually see it. Even under the sack, the air smelled mild. Where were they taking me, I wondered. And how long had I been in the cell?

I thought back. I had said ten sets of morning prayers.

———————————

We drove for a couple of hours. Every once in a while we stopped, and I could hear the policemen getting out for some tea. I could hear the spoons clinking in their glasses. They were laughing and shooting the breeze. I was left alone back in the car and had to listen to Pakistani pop music on the radio. That was a true punishment.

After about half a day, we arrived somewhere. Again I was led up some stairs. I heard a lot of doors. There were always steps, up and down, and then another door. A policeman put his arm out in front of my chest—a sign for me to stop walking and stand still.

Someone took the sack from my head. I found myself in a cell that was scarcely bigger than the one from which I'd been moved. But one of the walls was open. There were metal bars and behind them a hallway about three feet wide. Artificial light streamed in from somewhere.

A man was squatting Indian style in one corner of the room. The police released me from my chains and left the two of us alone.

About three feet in front of the other prisoner was a container about as big as a shoe box. It contained sweets, green, yellow, and red. Cookies.

Never before my life had I felt so hungry. For days all I had eaten were those red lentils. I wanted nothing more to pounce on the box of sweets.

"Salam alaikum," I said.

"Alaikum salam," said the man on the floor.

I could tell he was an Arab.

I asked him who he was and he answered in Arabic. I couldn't understand him. I sat down in another corner of the room. The man stared at the box. I stared at the box, too.

After a while, the Arab asked me if I wanted something to eat. At least, that was what I gathered from his hand gestures.

No, I signaled back. No, thank you.

The Arab put his hand to his mouth, nodding.

I should eat, he was trying to tell me.

I ate the entire box. I would have given all the money I have ever earned in my entire life for that one box of cookies.

Soon there would be four of us. Two Arabs were brought back to the cell. I discovered that they were being interrogated when I arrived. The man who gave me the sweets was from Bahrain. His name was Kemal. One of the other two men was from Oman, let's call him Salah. Today he's back home, but I don't want to him to get any trouble. I spent four years of my life with Salah. I saw him over and over again in different cellblocks in Guantanamo. Salah spoke very good English. He told me that he had gone to university in the United States. As of 2007, Kemal is still imprisoned at Guantanamo.

On the one hand, my situation had improved—at least I could make myself understood to Salah. On the other hand, things had definitely taken a turn for the worse. The cell was damp and cold, and it was crawling with cockroaches, beetles and strange, exotic spiders with fat bodies and hairy legs. There was no toilet, just a bucket. I soon got sick and started vomiting. Though our meals now consisted of rice and Pakistani bread as well as lentils, all I threw up was water or acidic yellow froth.

A piece of bread the size of a pita and a plate of rice or lentils twice a day—that's all the four of us were given to subsist on. We shared the food, but at some point I couldn't eat any more. It was strange, I was permanently hungry, but I couldn't eat anything. That was completely new to me. In Bremen, we fasted during the daytime during the month of Ramadan. But we filled our bellies in the morning and the evening. Your stomach might have grumbled in between, but it didn't hurt.

Now my stomach definitely hurt. I felt a constant burning, acidic sensation in the back of my throat. Everything hurt, my stomach, my throat, even my tongue, which had become heavy, swollen, and dry. After a few days, I started feeling weak and getting headaches. I couldn't sleep, and over time I found I didn't have enough strength to move.

But I could talk to Salah. I learned more English from him than in all the previous weeks I spent in Pakistan.

The Pakistanis interrogated me twice in this cell. They always asked the same questions. They photographed me and took my fingerprints.

What are you doing here? they asked.

Where do you come from?

What have you done?

Then they took me for my first interrogation with Americans.

We drove for a while by car through the city. I could hear the sounds of city streets, motorcycle rickshaws, and shouting in the marketplace. I was shackled and had a sack over my head. It was very hot. When we stopped, a policeman took the sack from my head so I could see the building we were about to enter. It was a large, brightly painted villa. Inside, it was cool—there was probably air conditioning. I was led through the house. There was a nice-looking salon with plants, armchairs and books, then a corridor, thick white wooden doors with windows in them, and high ceilings with spinning fans. I was taken to a room where I was told to wait. The policemen took their seats next to me on a bench.

After a short while the door opened, and an American came in and looked me over. He almost seemed startled. What had he expected? He was probably surprised that I looked so European. Even though I was dirty and unshaven, and my clothes were unwashed, I still had fair skin.

"The German guy!" he exclaimed.

Then a second American came in and examined me. Both of them were wearing civilian clothing, cotton pants and shirts. The second one also sported a V-neck sweater. He had salt-and-pepper hair and a moustache. He almost looked German.

I said, "I come from Germany. I'm German."

The two Americans exchanged smiles.

"Yeah, the German guy," said the one with the sweater.

The policemen motioned for me to get up and follow them. The two Americans took the lead, and we trotted along behind them. I was taken to an interrogation room where there were three chairs and a table. I was still wearing chains, and my guards stood holding machine guns. Maybe, I thought later, the Americans were afraid I was going to attack them. All I wanted was to ask them when I could go home. As far as I was concerned, Turkey would do. I still believed they just wanted to ask me some questions and would then let me go.

The man with the sweater rolled up his sleeves and began the interrogation. The questions were similar to the ones the Pakistani police kept asking me, but this time I could understand them better.

Name?

Age?

Profession?

When did you come to Pakistan?

All of that information was contained in the passport and the plane ticket they had in front of them.

Then the Americans wanted to know why I was in Pakistan. I tried to explain to them that I was a student of the Koran, that I had wanted to study at the Mansura Center in Lahore but had been turned down after being told it was too dangerous at the moment for them to accept foreigners because the Americans had just invaded Afghanistan. But I didn't say that.

At first I'd been upset about getting turned away by the Mansura Center. But I didn't want to turn around and go home, now that I was already here. I knew from some other *tablighis* in Bremen that Koran students in Pakistan move from mosque to mosque in small groups. I wanted to join these groups, I explained to the American.

He then wanted to know what I had been doing since the day I entered Pakistan, which was over two months before. I told him that I had traveled with other Koran students and that we had slept in the mosques, which we had gotten to know after praying there.

My English was still very bad. He didn't seem to understand a lot of what I was trying to say. But he understood enough to ask who these Koran students were, what their names were, and where they were now. I told him

I didn't know. There were always new students joining the groups, while others went their own way. But I could make myself understood. I told him about Mohammad, whom I hadn't seen since I had been forced to leave the bus at the checkpoint in Peshawar. Surely he had asked about me.

Then the American wanted to know where exactly I'd been in Pakistan.

"Karachi," I said. "Airplane: I landing. No speak language. Nobody speak English. I meet Hassan in the plane. Hassan is from Islamabad. So I go to Islamabad. But not with Hassan. Hassan take the airplane to Islamabad."

"So you went by bus or by train to Islamabad?" asked the American.

"Airplane. I buy new ticket and take the airplane, later. But in Islamabad I don't find Hassan. Telephone number he gave me—no good. I go to Lahore, to Masura Center for Islam. They say: no German, too dangerous. I go to Islamabad. I meet Mohammad. We sleep in the mosques. We study Koran. We study hadith. Hadith!"

One of the Pakistani policemen nodded.

"Then we take train to Peshawar."

What had I been doing in Bremen? asked the American.

I couldn't understand why he wanted to know that, but I answered anyway.

"I live in Bremen. I live in the house of my parents. I study ships, and then I study Koran. I marry Muslim woman from Turkey, so I want to study Koran."

Proudly I showed him the wedding band on my finger.

Suddenly, the American asked: "Are you a terrorist?"

"Terrorist? No, I'm German. I'm Turkish, but I live in Germany. I'm born in Germany, in Bremen."

"Do you know Osama?"

"No."

"Where is Osama? Tell me!"

"I don't know."

"Tell me and I'll let you go . . ."

"No! No! I don't know . . ."

─────────────

The Pakistani policemen brought me back to the cell with the others. We stayed there for several days. Then some Pakistani soldiers came. Their commander, perhaps a general, was short and stocky and brought us some blue overalls—a kind of prison uniform. We were forced to put them on. We weren't allowed to wear anything underneath. Our own clothes were taken away. Then they chained our hands and feet.

Salah and the others knew that we were to be handed over to the Americans. But they hadn't told me.

The general said, "*Mecburi. Mecburi.*" He looked me in the eye. Then he said in English, "Forgive me!"—before he put the sack over my head.

I'll never forgive him. Not even in the afterlife.

After we had gone up some stairs and had been loaded into a truck, the sack had slipped somewhat and I was able to nudge it further up without the soldiers noticing. I saw that we were in a military truck covered by a camouflaged tarpaulin. Suddenly a hand pulled the sack down over my eyes.

We only drove a short distance—probably no more than ten minutes. Then I heard airplanes, propeller-driven motors. I thought: they're taking me to Turkey. The planes' motors were already running. They were ready for takeoff. I heard other trucks that sounded just like the one we were in. Then I heard voices. American voices.

As we got out of the truck, I was able to push up the sack a little bit again. I saw lots of American soldiers in uniform, light-colored camouflage gear. I still thought they were going to take me to an American military base in Turkey. I was glad to be finally leaving Pakistan.

─────────────

They searched me—even though I was wearing nothing underneath my overalls and had nothing left to my name, not even a pair of shoes. I felt their hands everywhere, and they were rough. Someone grabbed my right hand and tugged at my ring finger. He's after my wedding ring, I thought, the ring inscribed with my wife's name. One of the soldiers tugged at it. I balled my hand and tried to make a fist, but I was too weak. I was too weak to offer much resistance, and my fingers had gotten thin. They pried my fingers apart, and the ring slipped off.

I heard a soldier throw the ring away.

It clattered on the asphalt.

I was enraged, but there was nothing I could say. I was half-starved and bound in chains. I could hardly stand on my own two feet, when a deafening sound almost knocked me over.

The sound of hydraulics. An airplane hatch being opened mechanically.

We were pushed inside. I felt cold, raw metal against the soles of my bare feet.

"Sit!" a GI screamed in my ear. "Sit! Sit down, motherfucker!"

I fell on my behind and cowered on the metal floor. The soldier pressed my head down. I heard yelling and shouting. It came from a large number of other prisoners in the plane.

Suddenly I felt a blow to my head. I fell over to one side and lay there. Then I received a kick to the stomach.

It was the first time I was beaten.

They kicked my arms, legs and back with their boots. I had no way of defending myself. All I could do was cower.

I didn't have the strength to scream. There was only one thought in my head: they're taking me to Turkey. They're taking me to a base in Turkey, where they'll hand me over to the Turks.

They chained me to the floor. Soon, I thought, it will be all over.

They kicked me in the back.

I heard the hydraulics. Commands were barked out. The loading hatch shut.

Soon it will be all over.

III

KANDAHAR, AFGHANISTAN

'D BEEN SOLD, FOR A BOUNTY OF $3,000, TO THE AMERICANS. That's what the Americans themselves told me in one of the endless interrogations in Guantanamo Bay. "I know," I told my interrogator, "you expected more for the $5,000 you paid for me."

"$3,000," said my interrogator. "We only paid $3,000 for you."

That's when I knew the story was true.

When I was apprehended, everyone knew that there was money to be made by turning in foreigners. Lots of Pakistanis were sold as well. Doctors, taxi drivers, fruit and vegetable sellers, many of whom I later met in Guantanamo. I don't care who got paid the reward money in my case. It could just as well have been the policeman at the checkpoint in Peshawar or the blond European or the American man at the villa. Maybe the officers at the police station in Peshawar split the money. $3,000 is a lot in Pakistan. A man can get married with a sum like that, or buy a car and an apartment.

Everyone, except me, knew about the reward money. I only discovered later that the Americans paid for us, as if we were slaves.

As the plane got ready to take off, not only were we shackled and chained, we were bound up like packages. I could hear the noise of the propeller and the shouts of the soldiers and the other prisoners. From beneath the sack covering my head, I could see a bit of the plane's aluminum wall. We were bound tightly to the walls with long belts so that we couldn't move the lower half of our bodies. My legs were stretched out straight and manacled. Chains constrained my feet above the ankles. The only thing I could move was my head.

On board the plane with me were the four other men from my cell and around twelve more prisoners. I couldn't see how many soldiers there were, but to judge from the confusion of voices, it must have been a lot. They went from one prisoner to the next, hitting us with their fists, their billy clubs, and the butts of their rifles. It was as cold as a refrigerator; I was sitting on bare metal and icy air was coming from a vent or a fan. I tried to go to sleep, but they kept hitting me and waking me.

"Keep your head up!" they'd yell.

They never let up hitting, kicking, and insulting us. Sometimes they'd forget about me for a couple of minutes, but then they'd strike me all the harder.

"You're terrorists," they shouted.

"We're Americans! You're terrorists. We've got you! We're strong! And we will give it to you!"

They never ceased screaming.

"You fuckers!"

Prisoners, I thought, are often beaten in Turkey. It's a well-known fact, and so it seemed almost normal to me that the Americans would do the same. If I had been put in a Turkish prison, they would have beaten me there as well. At some point, I also thought, this will be over. But the soldiers never tired of beating us, laughing all the while. I imagine they made jokes at our expense.

It was night when we took off, but the lights were on inside the plane. All I could see were my bare feet and the bright light. My thin overalls were no match for the cold, and my feet and hands had swollen from being tightly shackled. I was afraid I would never be able to use my hands again. I knew that a hand can die, if the blood flow is cut off, and that the skin can turn black from the cold. I watched my feet slowly turning dark blue. I couldn't feel them any more. All I could feel, throughout my entire body, was pain. I was barely able to breathe.

I didn't try to speak to any of the other prisoners. If you spoke, you would have been beaten even more, so none of us did. I was far too weak and hurting. I wasn't afraid. But it was clear to me that I might die. I didn't want to die, but in my situation it seemed like the easier option. Better. I thought about my family. If I was going to die, would someone tell them how my life ended and what had happened to me? Would my family be able to live with that? No doubt they had no idea where I was or what was happening to me. I thought above all about my mother. I hoped at least she would find out how I died.

I prepared myself for my death.

I didn't cry. I'd admit it if had, but I simply couldn't. Even our Prophet cried after the death of his son, but I couldn't cry in the plane. I believe we have a saying: The tears of the heart are worse than the tears of the eye. But maybe this isn't really a saying. Perhaps I invented it during the flight. In any case, I kept repeating the words: *Kalbin aglamasi gözlerin aglamasin dan cok daha siddetlidir.*

I quietly prayed for patience. Allah, give me patience and strength and protect me. I know you are The Most Excellent Protector, and I expect protection only from you because you are The Most Strong.

I said prayers like this for the next five years.

I don't know how long the flight lasted. At some point, we started our descent. I heard the motors cut back, and I knew the plane would land. Nothing can happened to me, I thought. I was strapped in tight.

I heard the hydraulics of the rear section of the plane opening. I felt a blow to my head, and as I stood up, I saw bright flashes through the sack. Flashbulbs. From beneath the sack, I could make out soldiers filming and photographing us. They were standing on the runway. I could look down at them from underneath the sack. They never entered the plane.

Suddenly I realized something. Just as they had repeatedly called us terrorists during the flight, they were taking photos to depict us as terrorists to the world. Either they truly believed I was a terrorist, or they knew I was innocent but needed scapegoats to proudly present to the public. That made me upset. They were going to say to America and the rest of the world: "These are the terrorists we've been hunting for. These are the criminals who are responsible for the attacks of September 11. Now we have them, and this is how they'll be treated!"

What I didn't know at the time was that the photos were to be used as "evidence" in the media that we had been captured in the war zone in Afghanistan by American soldiers—even though we had all been taken prisoner in Pakistan by Pakistani police. I discovered all this later when I faced the military tribunal in Guantanamo.

In the plane, I had only one thing on my mind: the singular mission of proving my innocence to my captors. The soldiers had to assume I was a terrorist, if that's what they had been told. If that was true, they had good reason to beat me. Although it was unjust, I could understand them. But one way or the other, so I thought back then, my innocence would be proven, and I would be released. It would only take a few days. I intended to clear up the situation at my next interrogation.

I felt a new sense of hope.

The soldiers loosened my restraints. When they lifted me up, I felt too weak to stand on my own two legs. They linked our arms together with a thin but robust strip of plastic. I was swaying on my feet, and then I felt something cut into my arm: the plastic band attaching me to the prisoners in front of and behind me. I sensed a dull ache as I took a few steps. It was like walking on something strange, like stilts, that burrowed into my body. But I was lucky. Other prisoners had broken legs. Some of them were trying to walk on one leg. Two soldiers dragged one of the prisoners across the floor of the airplane. I saw his foot bent at a severe angle at the ankle.

I heard dogs barking. We stumbled out of the plane down a ramp. Whenever someone fell, the plastic strip would drag me down as well. I heard dogs growling and barking. They were everywhere around us, and I could hear them biting. You can hear a dog's bite. They were German shepherds and Belgian shepherds, or malinois. Back in Bremen, I had had dogs, and I was able to recognize the breeds from beneath the sack. Malinois are bigger and stronger than German shepherds. They have shorter fur, and it's usually one color.

We walked for a few minutes and then they threw us to the ground. We were ordered to lie on our stomachs. A soldier sat on my back. My breath condensed under the sack. I felt the cold of the freezing stone ground. As far as I could understand what the soldiers were saying, they were going to come collect us one by one and take us away. I heard helicopters and the motors of jeeps and trucks. First one, then the next, then a third. It took a long time. I lay on the ground for what could have been hours, or minutes. Then I lost consciousness, probably because of the cold.

I woke up when someone hit me in the face.

"I feel his heartbeat again," said the soldier who had been sitting on my back.

It was my turn.

Someone picked me up, and I tried to walk. The soldier rammed his fist into my back, and I pressed forward until someone stopped me. The sack was removed from my head. I was in a tent. In front of me sat a man at a table with paper and a pen. Two soldiers cut open my overalls so that they wouldn't have to loosen my bonds. I was naked. I saw some other clothes, orange overalls, lying on a chair.

"Name?"

"Age?"

"Place of birth?"

Someone pulled out some of my hair. I was weighed, and a saliva sample was taken. Soldiers motioned for me to pick up the orange overalls. I heard shots outside and what I believed to be a bomb exploding. The man on the chair flinched at the sound. Then I was given the number 53. I was the fifty-third prisoner. There was another muffled bang. The same number was imprinted on the green plastic band that they fastened round my wrist. The soldiers seemed nervous.

"Hurry!"

I heard the unmistakable sounds of airplanes and battle. Rockets hissing and whistling, then muffled bangs on impact.

It was then that I realized I wasn't in Turkey, but in some sort of war zone.

"Hurry up!"

The Americans were being attacked, and they were returning fire. Planes and helicopters took off and landed. The impact sounds of the rockets were close. The man at the table looked pale.

"Look down!" he yelled.

I felt the soldiers' fear as they grabbed me by the arms. They pushed my head to the ground with all their might. It seemed to me that they were less afraid of the bombs than of me, although I was naked, bound and unarmed.

The officer asked me some more questions, but I wasn't able to answer them. I could hardly stand and lacked the strength for anything more than a yes or no. They led me back out of the tent.

It was night-time. I saw a barricade made of coiled, barbed wire. The barricade was out in the open in the middle of a pen, measuring about thirty-three by sixteen feet and was guarded by soldiers in groups of two. There was no door to the pen, only two poles on chains that were raised and lowered. Twenty to thirty prisoners crouched inside. A soldier hit me in the back of the head with the butt of his rifle. I fell to the ground.

"See that?!"

He motioned with his weapon.

"Can you see that?!" he yelled.

"Don't move!"

I understood. If I moved, he was going to shoot me. Other soldiers took off my restraints. When they removed the handcuffs, I found I could no longer move my fingers. They were dark blue and numb, as were my feet. They threw the overalls on the ground. I started to pick them up and put them on.

They pointed their rifles at me.

"Don't move!"

"Sit!" they yelled.

I sat down. Edging backwards, the soldiers began to exit the pen.

"Sit! Don't move!" they kept yelling, even after they were outside.

I was forced to remain seated like that, naked, with the overalls beside me, until the following day. I was terribly cold. After a while, I lay down. I was tired and fell asleep. I slept very well.

When morning broke, I looked around. I saw tents, barbed wire and a tall structure, perhaps a guard tower. The landing strip, where their planes and helicopters took off and landed, couldn't have been far away. There was a long hangar made of wood and corrugated metal as well as the frame of a second hangar. The metal of the first hangar was full of holes. Bullet holes, I thought.

Alongside the tents, I could see other open tents that consisted merely of olive-green tarpaulins on wooden poles. There were soldiers hammering and drilling everywhere. I saw bulldozers. The camp seemed to be still under construction. Next to the tower, I could make out a kind of wall made of metal, perhaps tin. It may have run all the way around the camp, but I couldn't see that far. In the distance, behind the hangars, there were white shafts that looked like crosses on graves. But they couldn't have been graves because the shafts were at least ten feet high. On the other side, somewhat at a distance, we could see a second barbed-wire pen with other prisoners.

The military camp was surrounded, as far the eye could see, by mountains. They were gigantic. I'd never seen so many mountains of that height. I was sitting in a camp in the desert surrounded by tall, silvery-gray mountains. There was snow on their peaks. The ground in the camp consisted of frozen soil that had been dug up like the rock bed of a dried-up river. I could still hear helicopters taking off and landing. Fog rolled in.

Some of the prisoners sitting on the ground were naked like me. Others had already put on overalls. Some of them were still wearing the rusty metal shackles from Pakistan, thick rings around their ankles with a bar in between. I noticed that the guards were occupied with a prisoner far off from me and quickly put on my overalls. They didn't say anything. I buried my chin beneath the material and blew my breath across my chest. That warmed me up a bit. I moved my hands, flexing them. But it would be days before the feeling returned to my fingers.

I tried talking to the others. We were forbidden from talking, but we did so anyway. Whenever the soldiers would stray from the barbed wire, we tried to exchange a few words. But I didn't know either Arabic or Farsi, the Afghan language, and my English was poor. I couldn't find Salah or any of the others from the prison in Pakistan. They must have been put in another pen. But I did discover that the Americans were using this as a base to fight the Taliban in the mountains. So we had to be somewhere in Afghanistan. Was this a former Russian airbase, perhaps? We talked in English as best we could, occasionally gesturing with our hands and feet. But that was conspicuous.

Some of the people in the pen were Arabs who lived in Afghanistan. Others were Arabs from Pakistan, taxi drivers or shopkeepers or small entrepreneurs. One was a doctor, so that's what we called him: the doctor. He, too, was a foreigner who had been sold to the Americans. He was in orthopedics. He communicated this by tapping on his elbows and knees. As far as I could gather, he had been brought here as part of the first group, twelve hours ahead of me. I was part of the second group that had come from Pakistan. If I interpreted his gestures correctly, this first group had been beaten even worse than we were.

I met the doctor again later in Guantanamo, and we spoke often. I asked him a lot of questions, including medical ones. He was indeed an orthopedist, as I had gleaned in Kandahar, and he was also an expert on nutrition. I found that interesting. I asked him what you should eat and not eat if you had broken a bone. What a layman should do to treat a broken bone and things like that. Broken bones were a constant threat in Guantanamo. The doctor had lived in Pakistan for twenty years. His children had grown up and gone to school there. Almost everyone in the city where he lived knew him. One night, the Pakistani police hauled him out bed. They kicked in the doors and broke the windows of his house, then entered his bedroom from every direction. He was tied up on the ground. His wife and children were terrified. He had been imprisoned for a while in Pakistani jails, then they handed him over to the Americans, claiming he was a terrorist who had worked together with other terrorists. But it was really only about the reward money.

I didn't care about anything on this particular morning. I was hungry and I had to go to the toilet. But there was no toilet.

I tried to ask one of the soldiers on guard.

"Toilet, toilet," I said.

"Shut up! Sit down!"

He pointed his gun at me.

I couldn't sit down because I had to go so badly. I just didn't care anymore. I approached the barbed wire. The soldier yelled at me, as though he was about to shoot me.

I ignored him and let it all out.

The soldier disappeared and returned a few moments later, accompanied by an officer. The officer was carrying a blue plastic bucket. He threw it over the barbed wire and said we could use it. Almost all the prisoners got up and made use of the bucket. It was humiliating. Whether we were young or old, religious or not—we all had to strip naked to do our business in the bucket because we were wearing nothing but overalls.

Men like me who follow the rules of Islam are forbidden from exposing our bodies between the navel and the knees. It's also prohibited in the *hamam* or Turkish bath. Even in my fitness club back in Bremen, I used to shower with my shorts on.

Female guards also patrolled the grounds outside our pen. It wasn't easy.

We sat the entire day in the pen. Other groups of prisoners were locked in with us and in the other pens. They, too, were naked and initially had to leave their overalls lying beside them. I'd estimate the total number of prisoners at around sixty.

At sunset, soldiers would come and lead us away in groups of about ten. On average, the way this happened was that about a dozen soldiers would enter the pen waving machine guns. We stood up one by one and approached the barbed wire. Our hands and feet were bound, and they led us to the hangar. The hangar was empty—there were no planes. All I could see was a long corridor, a number of pens with walls of corrugated metal, topped by barbed wire. We were herded toward the spaces enclosed by the metal walls and made to lie on the ground. It consisted of sand, rocks, and frozen soil just like our pen. The space was locked from the outside. Each of us received an MRE in a plastic container, which was thrown over the barbed wire.

MRE stands for "Meal Ready to Eat." Pronounced in Arabic, the acronym sounds like "Emarie," so that's what we called the packages. They were supposed to contain approximately 2,000 calories. Typically, they contained food like potatoes packed in tin foil or rice, meat or chicken, some vegetables and pudding, porridge, crackers and something sweet. The forks, spoons and knives were made of plastic. There was also a small flameless heater to warm the food up. Each Emarie was numbered from 1 to a number above 30. Some of them contained pork. The Emaries that they threw over the barbed wire for us only contained a bit of rice or porridge and a couple of pieces of meat, all mashed together. The other food had been removed from the plastic containers, leaving less than 600 calories. Human beings need more than 1,500 calories a day to survive. I knew that from my training as a fitness coach in Bremen.

My first Emarie happened to contain pork. The word was written on the side of the package. It was just a couple of cold, dried-out pieces of pork in rice. But I couldn't eat pork because it's against my religion so I tried to get something else. I got up, went to the barbed wire and attempted to speak to one of the soldiers.

"Shut up!" he yelled at me.

I warmed up my food.

In Bremen, I competed in a few boxing tournaments. I used to give karate lessons and had worked as a bouncer. When I looked at the guards, I knew that I could have any of them on the ground within a couple of seconds. That made me even more enraged. There was a soldier behind a wall of barbed wire who, despite his machine gun, seemed to be afraid of me and kept yelling at me. But he had the right to abuse me. Maybe it sounds immature when I describe my nineteen-year-old rage in this situation. Other people may see things differently. But for me it was hard to swallow.

I took a seat back on the ground and ate the crackers.

One of the younger prisoners had witnessed the scene. He edged over to me and offered to share his Emarie. I tried to refuse, but he insisted. The word "chicken" was printed on the side of his Emarie. I realized then that there were good people among the prisoners. In a situation like this, food is all you have, your sole possession. And although he was hungry, this young man still found it within him to share his food with me. He couldn't have been more than sixteen—he didn't even have a beard. But he had a good heart.

Then the door in the barbed wire opened. The soldiers hit the boy for sharing his food with me.

That was difficult for me to watch.

I never saw the boy again. Maybe he is dead. Or perhaps I simply didn't recognize him in Cuba. Torture changes people.

That night we were moved. We were led away in groups of twenty to a new barbed-wire pen, holding about sixty of us. I tried to go to sleep, but that was the night of my first interrogation. Two soldiers came into the pen.

The Americans called them the "escort team."

I knew the word escort from my time in Bremen as a bouncer at clubs. It referred to women who accompanied gentlemen for an evening. Now I was being taken away by escorts. It was always the same procedure.

They would call my number.

"Zero Five Three, get ready!"

I would lie down on my stomach near the entrance to the pen, my hands behind my back. Everyone else would get up and go to the opposite side of the pen, their faces turned toward the barbed wire. The escort team then stormed in and put me in handcuffs and shackles. One of them punched me in the back with his fist. The other picked me up in his arms. One of them grabbed my hair from behind and pushed my head down. I was frog-marched out.

I was led to a tent. There were several officers there. They spoke to me in English, although I hardly knew two words of the language. They asked:

"Where is Osama?"

"Are you part of Al Qaeda?"

"Are you a Taliban?"

That's as much I could understand.

They kept repeating the same questions.

"Are you part of Al Qaeda?"

"No."

One of the soldiers punched me in the face.

"Are you a Taliban?"

"No."

The soldier punched me again.

"Where is Osama?"

"I don't know."

The other soldier punched me, this time square on the chin.

"Are you part of Al Qaeda?"

"No . . ."

Another punch to the face. My lips were split, and blood was dripping from my nose.

"Are you a Taliban?"

"No!!!"

Every time I said no, they hit me.

"Do you know Mohammed Atta?" one of the officers suddenly asked.

The name seemed familiar. I thought it over. My head was pounding. Where have I heard this name before, I asked myself. Everything was spinning.

"One moment," I said. "Yes, I know. I hear. That name. I don't know where . . ."

Then I remembered. In the news. It was the name of the man accused of masterminding the attacks on September 11. I tried to explain in English.

"Yes," I understood the officer as saying. "He was a friend of yours."

"What?"

"He was your friend!"

"No, I only know him from the news . . ."

I felt the next blow.

"TV! TV! News! You understand?"

"You're friends with him!"

"No . . ."

The officer got up. I was kneeling on the ground, my hands bound behind my back. The officer came up and punched me in the face. He wasn't old, maybe in his early thirties. He asked me what I was doing in Pakistan. I told him, as best I could, about the *tablighis* and Mohammed. He yelled: "You're lying! Your visa is a fake!" I replied: "You can check it. You've got it!" He went back to the table and picked a file off the ground.

He emptied out the contents on the table's surface. It was my wallet, my plane tickets, my passport, and my German identity card.

"There," I said. "Look in my passport. My visa is in there."

He examined my passport.

"It's faked," he said.

He showed me the stamp from the consulate.

"You made that yourself."

"Call them up. I got it from the Pakistani consulate in Germany. I was there! Why would I fake my visa?"

"You wanted to go to Afghanistan!"

"No"—the next blow came down.

"You know Osama!"

"No, no! Call Germany! Call my mother, my school . . ."

"Where is Osama?"

"No, no . . ."

He punched me.

"You're a Taliban!"

"No, no . . ."

He punched me.

Suddenly the American asked me about a name I do know. It was the name of a friend of mine from school. He recited a number but I didn't understand. Was it a telephone number?

"Zero-zero-four-nine-four-two-one . . ."

"I know . . . friend! He's a friend from school!"

He recited a second name. It was a friend of mine from the mosque in my home district of Hemelingen in Bremen. Again he read out a number, first the name, then a number from a piece of paper.

"Yes, I know, friend . . ."

He repeated the numbers. I made out the area code for Bremen and a couple of the other digits. How did he get these telephone numbers?

"Fatima. Zero-zero-nine-zero . . ." the American said.

"My wife! My wife! In Turkey . . ."

Suddenly he asked:

"You sold your cell phone before you left Germany. Why did you sell your cell phone?"

That I understood. It was true. I had sold my mobile before I'd flown to Pakistan.

"Yes! I sell handy. How you know?"

"Handy" is the German word for cell phone. He punched me in the face.

"Who did you sell it to?"

I couldn't remember. I was always purchasing the latest cell phone and selling off my old one. Was it to a second-hand electronics store? Or to one of my buddies? I didn't know. But I did sell it. That much was true . . .

I felt a blow to the back of my head.

"I don't know . . . I always sell handy . . ."

I asked myself: How does he know these things? But I didn't have time to ponder the question because someone was hitting me again. I saw stars.

"You took money from your bank," the officer said. "1,100 German Marks from Bremen Bank. I know that. What did you use it for?"

The only words I understood are Bremen Bank. That was my bank. How did he know that? I hadn't brought my ATM card to Pakistan!

"Quick! Answer! What did you use that money for?"

Money?

"1,100 German Marks!"

"Ticket! I buy ticket to Pakistan and back!"

"Who is Selcuk Bilgin?"

Selcuk? How did he know about Selcuk? I never told anyone about Selcuk. Why would I have? They wouldn't have understood . . .

"Quick!"

I felt a kick to the stomach. I collapsed, thinking I was going to be sick.

"Friend! My friend! Together to Pakistan . . . but no come . . ."

Hour upon hour, they repeated the same questions accompanied by punches and kicks. It was no use. The officer simply refused to understand who I was and what I intended to do with Selcuk in Pakistan. We wanted to go to Koran school. I had waited for Selcuk for days at the airport in Karachi, but he never arrived, as he had promised he would in Frankfurt. It was no use. The officer wasn't listening. He just asked the same questions and recited the same names and numbers, and then they hit me. I don't know how long I was interrogated that day. But I can still remember the words he kept repeating.

"You're a terrorist! We know that. We're going to keep you forever. You're never going home!"

When I regained my senses, I was back in the pen. My face was swollen, and every bone in my body ached. I heard them call out the number of another prisoner. The escort team came and led him away.

The escort team was always coming and going from the pen, bringing someone back or taking someone away for interrogation. I, too, was interrogated again that first day. Or was it the next morning? In any case it had been dark for a while. It was always the same game with a different officer asking the questions and different soldiers hitting me. Names, numbers, accusations, blows. By the time I got back to the pen, I could never remember a thing.

But I tried to concentrate. How did they know the names and telephone numbers of my friends? Where did they get Selcuk's name? Then it occurred to me. Germany and the United States were allies! They probably cut a deal. They probably called up the German authorities. There was no reason for them not to. They probably called up and said: We've got someone here from Germany, and we'd like some information about him. Who is he?

That's how I imagined it. But if they knew that I'd sold my mobile phone, surely they'd also know I was innocent. They might have gotten the telephone numbers and the names from my cell phone. Maybe they were still saved there. I had saved the names of my friends and relatives, my brother-in-law and my sister in Bremen's Sebaldsbrück district. They could have also gotten many of the names from business cards in my wallet. All my friends in Bremen had business cards. I had many of these cards in my wallet, from colleagues from work and school friends. It doesn't cost much to have them printed.

But they also knew the name of one of *tablighis* from Bremen. I didn't have his business card. Of course, they knew who I was! It had been several days since the American had interrogated me in Peshawar. Surely they had gotten in touch with the relevant authorities in Germany to check that everything I was saying was true! That I came from Germany, that I wanted to visit a Koran school, that I was an apprentice ship-builder . . . but that would also mean that the German authorities had called my family and Selcuk. They must have found out that I wasn't a terrorist! I heard a number being called. It wasn't mine.

The following day, I was interrogated three times for about one and two hours each time. In between interrogations, I sat in the pen. It was bitterly cold. I could hardly feel my toes, which were still blue. Sometimes I thought back on how my mother used to bring me warm socks when she went to the shopping mall in Bremen. I hated wearing thick woolen socks with my sneakers. They were itchy. But when I thought of those socks, it was enough to drive me half-crazy. How nice it would have been to have a pair of those woolen socks now.

At the appointed hours of the day, we prayed, guessing the time from the position of the sun: in the morning, when it was getting light but still before sunrise; at noon, when the sun was at its peak; in the evening, after sunset but before it had gotten completely dark; and at night. Each of us prayed on his own, either quietly or silently, and we remained seated.

Early one morning, when we prayed together for the first time, they threatened to shoot us. But we kept on praying. If they wanted to shoot us, we thought, let them shoot. They didn't. They just yelled and made threats. Then a commander or some high-ranking officer came and spoke to us. He said we would be allowed to pray at the appointed times. Not because he wanted to do us any favors, but because he realized that we would rather die than not say our prayers. And they didn't want us to die because they still needed to interrogate us. From then on, we started our prayers standing, then knelt down and bowed our heads toward the East. We weren't able to wash our hands, but our faith allows us to wash with sand if there isn't any water—it's called *teyamum*. We cleansed our hands with sand.

When it rained, the water would sting our faces and skin like needles. Everything turned to mud. The ground was pure sludge, and you felt you might get washed away in the mud and the water. Often we'd huddle together to keep warm. Then the rain would stop, the wind would kick up again, and the cold would creep into my head. The ground froze. My overalls remained wet and clammy. I could even see the cold. I saw it in the thick gloves, jackets and overcoats worn by the soldiers and the face masks they had under their motorcycle helmets. Their entire faces were covered by the masks, with mere slits for their eyes.

We weren't allowed to get up and move around except for prayers, no matter how badly we froze. But we could hardly move anyway because we were so undernourished. There were weaker, older men in the pen. Men with broken feet, men whose legs and arms were fractured or had turned blue, red, or yellow from pus. There were prisoners with broken jaws, fingers and noses, and with terribly swollen faces like mine.

In the evening, we were herded into the hangar and given an Emarie. In the morning, we were given some Afghan white bread—one loaf to be split among five prisoners. They simply threw the loaves of bread over the barbed wire. Sometimes they'd land in the dirt. Then the soldiers would throw plastic bottles of water over the barbed wire. A half-liter per person, per day. Sometimes they didn't give us any water or any bread. One morning we were all given blankets. From then on we were allowed to use the blankets for a couple of hours. Then we had to hand them back or leave them lying on the ground next to us.

At night we had no blankets. But in any case there was little opportunity to sleep. The soldiers came at night and made us stand for hours on end at gunpoint. Every prisoner was interrogated at least once a day. Interrogations also took place at night. We had to stand up and sit down. There were interrogations and beatings. Then we'd have to sit down and stand up again. When we were allowed to use the blankets, I would pull mine up over my head. After a while, my breath would warm the air underneath. But the blanket would get clammy and moist, and the moisture would freeze.

We hardly had a moment of rest. When I was lucky, I could lie down for half an hour. My breath froze on my overalls. Sometimes I asked myself which was better: the interrogations and beatings in the tents, or crouching around outside in the pen, where every few minutes we had to get up and line up against the barbed wire. At least it was warm in the tents. But you also had to deal with the uncertainty. Many people never came back from the interrogations. Had they been brought somewhere else? If so, where?

One time when the escort team came, the soldiers were carrying a long crate that looked like a coffin. But there were holes in it. They called out a number, and the rest of us had to line up against the barbed wire. I bent my head and peeped over my shoulder. The prisoner whose number had been called was lying on his stomach. The soldiers bound him, picked him up and put him in the crate. I heard them speaking to one another, but I only understood isolated words: *dangerous* and *caution*. They were saying the man was dangerous. They used belts inside the crate to tie the prisoner up like a package. Then they put down the lid and took him away.

That was how it went, day in, day out.

Nonetheless, I still hoped that I would get an interrogator whom I could convince of my innocence. I still thought they would find out that I had gotten married shortly before my trip, that my visa was legitimate, that I'd never been to Afghanistan, and that I was training to become a shipbuilder. A few more calls to Germany and they would find this out, and then they'd send me back home.

But every time I was brought to interrogation, they didn't listen to me, and I only understood a fraction of what they were saying and asking anyway. I could only answer the things I had understood. Often they acted as if I spoke perfect English. They even said sometimes, You speak perfect English. We know you do. Don't try to fool us. I recognized some of the officers who interrogated me. Then there would be new faces. But the interrogations were all the same. They recited the names and telephone numbers of my friends and tried to get me to admit to being a Taliban. They hit me and tried to get me to say: "Yes, I'm a Taliban," or "Yes, I'm from Al Qaeda" or "Yes, I know where Osama is." That was all they were interested in hearing.

I had no chance. My only hope was that someone from the German authorities or the German military would turn up.

We changed pens almost every day, moving from one barbed-wire enclosure to the next, and finally to ones that the soldiers had built under tarpaulin roofs. About two weeks after I arrived in the camp, I met a couple of Turkish men. Finally I could make myself understood and understand what someone else was saying. It was like salvation. And not only did they speak my language, they could also speak some Arabic, so they were well-informed about practically everything. I learned a lot from them. Where I was, what was going to be done with us, and who the Americans thought we were.

The Turks said we were in Kandahar.

I asked how they knew that. The camp could have been anywhere. All we could see were mountains!

They said the Afghans knew exactly what region we were in. I had no doubts any more. At least I've seen another country, I thought bitterly, and I didn't even have to pay for the trip.

I knew the two Turks had been taken prisoner in Pakistan just as I had. They told me. I didn't ask where and how that had happened, or what they were doing there. You don't ask things like that in a detention camp. The Americans asked us every day where and how we were captured and what business we had in Pakistan. If you came back and asked your fellow prisoners the same questions, you quickly got a reputation as a spy. Then you would have been shunned. In all those years, I always behaved the same way. I listened if someone wanted to tell me something, but I didn't ask any funny questions. The two Turks have since been released from Guantanamo. I'd like to see them again. To protect them, I'm going to call them Erhan and Serkan.

One day, people from the International Red Cross came to the camp and stood in front of our pen. Some of the prisoners went up to them and spoke with them. One of them was German. He addressed me in English, and when I explained where I was from, we switched over to German. He asked me if I wanted to write a letter to my family so that they would know where I was. Of course I wanted to. The German had long hair. He had a moustache, wore glasses, and was probably in his mid-forties.

He told me I wasn't allowed to write the letter myself. That was against the rules. I had to speak to him very loudly to make myself heard over the noise of the fighter jets landing and taking off. He stood in front of the barbed wire, paper at the ready, and I dictated a few lines to him. To the best of my recollection, this is what I said.

> *My dear family,*
>
> *I'm sure I've caused you a lot of worry. I'm sorry for that. I can't write myself—as you can see, this is not my handwriting. I am currently imprisoned at an American military base in Kandahar, Afghanistan. They're trying to make me out to be a terrorist. I don't know what the future holds. Every day we are beaten, but I'll get through it. I hope we'll see each other soon. Forgive me for all the trouble and worry I've caused you.*
>
> *Your son, Murat*

I gave the man my address and my parents' telephone number in Bremen. I told him that the German authorities must have already known that I was here. If the letter reached its destination, my parents would learn where I was—in case the authorities hadn't informed them yet. Maybe they could do something from Germany. And in case it was too late by then, at least my mother would know for certain how I had died.

That same evening, the escort team came and brought me to be interrogated. The officer held my letter in his hand. He showed it to me and then hit me. He said:

"That kind of stupid letter will never get to your home . . ."

I understood that clearly.

"We're not stupid," the officer explained. "If you want to write a letter home, you have to write it differently. 'I'm doing fine. I feel all right. Don't worry.' That sort of thing, you understand?"

Of course, they weren't stupid. I shouldn't have written anything about torture or anything like that. But I had hoped that the man from the Red Cross would be humane enough to call my parents.

The officer tried to begin the interrogation. I said nothing. I didn't say a word that evening, no matter how often they hit me.

Today I know that the man from the Red Cross never called my parents. I also know he was forced to sign papers, agreeing not to pass on any information to the outside world, and that he had no choice but to agree to the conditions of the Americans, the rules of the camp. The only information that made it out of the camp was what they released. Nothing could be repeated, even orally, as another Red Cross representative explained to me later in Guantanamo. I never saw the German man who didn't call my mother again. Perhaps he took his work very seriously. Maybe he didn't want to lose his job. But I ask myself: Doesn't a person have a duty to help a fellow human being in a situation like that?

―――――――――――

Again I was moved, put together with different prisoners and taken to be interrogated. The escort team brought me to one of the tents. There they told me to sit on the ground with my legs stretched out. I didn't understand and tried to kneel as always. But they said: Sit! Sit down! Then they pushed my legs to the ground. I was to stretch them out. Two soldiers held my feet tight. Others grabbed my hands and pushed on my shoulders so that I could no longer move.

"So, you're not a terrorist?" one of the interrogators asked. "You're not from Al Qaeda?"

I could tell from his tone of voice that they were trying a new approach.

"Today we're going to find out," said another interrogator.

Did they have a lie detector? I asked myself. The man was holding something in his hands. It looked like two irons that he was rubbing together. Or one those machines used to revive people who have heart attacks. Before I realized what was happening, I felt the first jolt.

It was electricity. An electroshock.

They put the electrodes to the soles of my feet. There was no way to remain seated. It was as though my body was lifting itself off the ground of its own accord. I felt the electric current running through my entire body. There was a bang. It hurt a lot. I felt warmth, jolts, cramps. My muscles cramped up and quivered. That hurt, too.

"Did you change your mind?"

"What?"

I don't know how long they held the electrodes to the soles of my feet. It could have been ten or twenty seconds, maybe longer. It felt like an eternity.

"So how is that?"

The man rubbed the electrodes together and again touched them to my feet. Again I felt the cramps, the tremors, the hot pain.

"Funny, huh?"

The electricity crackled like a series of caps being hit with a hammer. They were like little bolts of lightning in my ear. If I could look inside my ear, I thought, there would electricity there—you could see electricity. At the same time, I heard screams.

They were my screams. But it seemed as though they were coming from outside my body, as though I had nothing to do with them. My whole body was quivering.

"Did you change your mind?"

"No, no . . ."

"Okay, try this!"

I heard myself screaming.

"Do you remember now who you are?"

"No, yes, no . . ."

"Okay, how about that . . ."

I heard my heart. It was beating loudly and very strangely. Quickly and then slowly again.

"Do you know Osama?"

"You . . . Taliban . . .?"

". . . Atta . . ."

I could hardly hear the man any more. I thought I was either going to pass out or die. But he always removed the electrodes from my feet. That was the worst thing, knowing that the pain would come again, until you thought there was no way you could take it any more.

I think I passed out. That was probably when they stopped.

It was night. I had been able to get some sleep, when suddenly I was awakened by screams. They came from some distance, from the second, open hangar, which was nothing more than a metal frame. I saw two soldiers hitting a man who was lying amidst some chain-link fencing on the ground. I could see that the prisoner's head had been wrapped in a blanket. The soldiers hit the man's head with the butts of their rifles and kicked him with their boots. Other guards and soldiers came up and started hitting and kicking him, too. There were now seven of them.

There were around a hundred feet between our pen and the open hanger. I noticed that the man was no longer moving. The soldiers kept kicking him. Then they walked away, leaving him lying there. Why, I asked myself, hadn't they chained him up and brought him back to his pen?

The next morning, the prisoner was still lying on the ground. I could now see that his head was completely wrapped in the blanket. How could he breathe, I asked myself. He was lying in a pool of blood.

That afternoon I saw four officers come and inspect him. They took notes. A short time later the escort team arrived. They unwrapped the blanket from his head, picked him up and put him on a stretcher—without restraining him. His arms and legs dangled lifelessly.

He was dead.

We all knew he was dead.

I wondered to myself if he had any children. Whether his mother and father would ever find out that he had been beaten to death. At that moment, I didn't care whether it was him or me. My life was worth nothing more than his. I'd understood for quite some time what this camp was about. They could do with us what they pleased. And I might be next.

———————

I entered the tent. What were they going to do to me now? They hadn't used electroshocks during my last few interrogations. They'd hit me as always, but that was it. At least it was warm in the tents.

On the table, there was a shallow, blue plastic bucket about 20 inches in diameter, full of water. I didn't know the interrogator. There were three officers there to ask me questions, with two soldiers as guards and assistants.

"So you still don't want to tell the truth," said one of the officers. "We will make you talk."

I knew what was coming.

They pushed my head into the plastic tub.

It's like bobbing for apples, I thought. Back in grade school in Hemelingen we had bobbed for apples at the school parties our teachers organized. It was a simple game. There was an apple floating in a bucket of water, you put your hands behind your back and tried to fish it out using only your teeth. Whoever succeeded first, won the game. But there was no apple in this bucket.

I wasn't afraid, but I was very nervous. I didn't know whether I was going to survive. I thought of something I'd learned with the *tablighis* at the mosques in Pakistan. It was the words of the prophet Abraham as he was about to be cast into the flames. *Habe allahu we ne emel wekil*: He is your Protector. What a splendid Protector.

Someone grabbed me by the hair. The soldiers seized my arms and pushed my head underwater.

In Islam, there is an idea that anyone who is forced to suffer a death by drowning will be given a great reward in the afterlife because it's a difficult way to die. I tried to think about that, while they held my head under water. Drowning is a horrible way to die.

They pulled my head back up.

"Do you like it?"

"You want more?"

"You'll get more, no problem."

When my head was back underwater, I felt a blow to my stomach. I had to exhale and cough. I wanted to breathe back in but forced myself not to, and I suppressed the urge to cough. Still, I inhaled a bit of water and could hardly hold my breath.

"Where is Osama?"

"Who are you?"

I tried to speak but I couldn't.

"More!"

I felt blows to my stomach and against my back. I swallowed some water. It was a strange feeling. I don't know whether the water went to my lungs. It became harder and harder to breathe, the more they hit me in the stomach and pushed my head underwater. I felt my heart racing. They didn't let up. I tried to answer their questions when I managed to get a breath of air, but all I could manage was "yes" and "no." I was choking. I felt like I was going to vomit, then I coughed and spat. I was dizzy and nauseous.

When they pushed my head under again and hit me in the stomach, I imagined myself screaming underwater.

Habe allahu we ne emel wekil!

I would have told them everything. But *what* was I supposed to tell them?

"I . . . don't know . . ."

The prophet Abraham didn't feel the flames.

Back in the pen, I spoke to another prisoner who had also been subjected to the waterboarding treatment. He said he had swallowed lots of water. He gestured, as though he were shoveling something into his mouth with his hand. Then he rubbed his belly to show how swollen it had been.

We couldn't help laughing.

The next morning, the escort team came yet again.

"053, get ready!"

I was being summoned for interrogation.

They led me to the hangar where we were usually given the Emaries. What was I doing here, I asked myself. They took me down a long corridor, then opened a door made of corrugated aluminum and pushed me inside. It wasn't a room, just a pen enclosed by aluminum and chain-link fence. Hanging from a beam was a hook like the ones used in butcher shops. A chain dangled from the ceiling.

The soldiers took the chain and ran it underneath my handcuffs. They looped the chain over the hook like a block and tackle and fed it into a winch. I was hoisted up until my feet no longer touched the ground. They clamped the chain to the beam and then left without a word, shutting the corrugated aluminum door behind them.

The cuffs cut off the blood to my hands. I tried to move. I tensed my shoulders, hunched my head into my neck and swung my legs. I tried to climb up the chain. I raised my legs and was able to maintain that position for a while. But then I had to lower them and wait. I relaxed my muscles. You can't fight against something like this for long. No one has that sort of strength.

I knew they were going to leave me hanging there until I couldn't take it any more. After a while, the cuffs seemed like they were cutting my wrists down to the bone. My shoulders felt like someone was trying to pull my arms out of their sockets. I tried to breathe evenly to conserve energy.

At some point, I began rocking myself back and forth in the hope that would get my blood flowing. But every movement hurt, no matter how tiny. Especially in my wrists and elbows. The best thing was just not to move and resign yourself to the pain. All I could do was let go. But letting go is impossible when you're under that much strain. I know now that people can die from this sort of treatment. Their bodies just can't take it.

At some point, hours later, someone came and let me down. A doctor examined me and took my pulse. He was wearing a uniform like the other soldiers, but he had a badge of rank on his shoulders, and a patch on his chest said: "Doctor."

"Okay," he said.

The soldiers hoisted me back up.

Three times a day, the soldiers came with the doctor and lowered me. In the morning, in the afternoon, and at night. At least I think it was morning, afternoon, and night.

I began to ask myself which was worse: bobbing for apples or being strung up from the ceiling.

At some point, someone came and started asking me questions. I could hardly understand him, but I already knew what he was asking. My answer was no.

My hands had swollen. In the beginning, I'd felt pain in them. Later on, I lost all feeling in my arms and hands. I still felt pain in other parts of my body, like in my chest around my heart.

When the interrogator arrived, they would lower me for a while. He would ask me if I had anything to say, whether I had changed my mind or had a different story to tell. But I could no longer speak.

The next time they lowered me, I could no longer stand. My legs buckled as if they were matchsticks, and I fell to the ground. The doctor examined my fingernails. My fingers were blue, and I felt a stabbing sensation. A stethoscope was hanging from his neck. He took my blood pressure. I could no longer feel anything in my hands at all—even the stabbing sensation had gone away. He pulled a penlight from his shirt pocket and shined it in my eyes.

I was no longer capable of answering, even if he had asked something. I couldn't understand a thing. I didn't even know whether he was saying anything in the first place. After he left, they hoisted me back up again. The doctor only seemed to be interested in how long I could stand this treatment. At some point, I didn't even register when he was there. I could only remember his visits because afterward I was hoisted up again. I could feel that, and I would open my eyes again. I don't know how long I lay on the ground in the intervals.

A lot of the time, it felt like I was falling asleep.

When they hung me up backwards, it felt as though my shoulders were going to break. They bound my hands behind my back and hoisted me up. I could remember seeing something like that in a movie once—only in the film, it was Americans being strung up by Vietnamese with their hands behind their backs until they died. I'm an athletic guy, I thought. Maybe I could pull up my legs and flip over so that I'd be hanging forward. But I was too weak.

I woke up when they hoisted me back up. I think it was a different day. This time, they hoisted me up higher than usual. Then they just left me dangling there. Before, my feet had been fifteen inches from the ground, now it was a good yard. Previously I had heard how they had hoisted up another prisoner on the other side of the aluminum wall, and I had seen the chains on the adjacent beam. Now I could see over the wall.

I didn't recognize the man. He was hanging as I was from the ceiling. I couldn't tell whether he was dead or alive. His body was mostly swollen and blue, although in some places it was pale and white. I could see a lot of blood in his face, dark streams of it. His head lolled to one side. I couldn't see his eyes.

I hardly moved, but once in a while I tried to swing myself back and forth a bit, even though it hurt. Just to do something. Several times a day, they lowered and examined me, then hoisted me back up. But no one came to lower the man next to me. They had forgotten him. He just hung there in the same position. I thought about the prisoner with the blanket wrapped around his head. They didn't seem to care whether we died. That man is dead, I thought. He looked like someone who had frozen to death in the snow.

I watched his chest for a while. Nothing moved. There's no way to survive if you're never taken down. I assumed the worst. That was something I learned over the years. Always assume the worst. Because that's how it's going to be.

And that's how it was.

———————————

I was strung up for about five days. As far as I could tell, it must have been between a minimum of four and a maximum of five days. Other prisoners in my pen told me it had been five days. I didn't think I would make it. I kept thinking, I can't take any more. Every person has his limits, and I often believed I had reached mine.

Today I know that a lot of inmates died from treatment like this. Other prisoners also saw our fellow prisoners die from being strung up. In Guantanamo, rumors went around that many people had died this way in Bagram, another U.S. military base in Afghanistan. Almost all of the prisoners at Guantanamo had been held first in either Bagram or Kandahar. And there were many people in Kandahar who never returned to their pens after being interrogated.

Later, my lawyers told me that some of the prisoners who disappeared had been set free while others had simply never been heard from again. Sometimes, you would see someone you thought was long dead. One of them was Yassir, an Arab American I met in Kandahar. I didn't know he was in Guantanamo, although we both spent time in solitary confinement in the same cell block. At the end of my imprisonment there, I learned from my American attorney that he had been freed. What's more, not all prisoners were tortured with the same intensity. They carefully selected certain prisoners to be treated especially harshly.

For example, Dilawar. He was a taxi driver from Afghanistan. There was talk that he had been transporting a generator in his car, and when they stopped him, they accused him of using it to fire rockets. They hung him up and beat him until he died. He probably died of thirst.

Thinking back on my time in Kandahar, I can't cry, and when I talk to someone who was in Guantanamo, we laugh about it. We laugh a lot— about how we were beaten and how we used to listen to one another screaming. What else are we supposed to do? Sit down and cry? It happened, and now it's over. Either I talk about it seriously, or I feel like I have to laugh. So I laugh. But I haven't forgotten a thing.

It's strange. I'm sitting here in my room, and everything is the same as when I was thirteen: the CDs I used to listen to are still on the shelf, Tupac and Snoop Dogg. The same curtains hang in the windows, my model boat is on the window sill, and my barbells are on the floor. It's as though I never got any older. When I first returned to my room, after being imprisoned for five years, I ate some mandarin oranges. Mandarins are good. I sit here and think about Kandahar, and I feel at home. I'm well fed, and the house is warm. I can eat and drink. Everything is here.

But I've learned that pain is part of life. That's the way life is.

When they finally took me off the hook, I lay on the ground for two days. I slept as much as possible. I hadn't eaten anything and hardly had anything to drink. Sometimes they offered me something to drink, but they'd just pour the water over my head and laugh. Once they stuffed an apple in my mouth and told me to eat. But I couldn't eat, and the soldiers laughed.

Then the escort team came and brought me back to the pen. It was raining. I lay down in the mud. I could still hardly move, and I fell asleep. At some point I had to go the toilet. I went to the bucket.

Then a woman came. Female soldiers often came and watched when we went to the toilet. We had to remove our overalls almost completely to use the bucket. It was humiliating. The women cracked stupid jokes about our private parts.

About fifteen soldiers, approximately one-third of them women, patrolled in shifts. It was only the women, not the men, who said anything, when we went to the toilet. I tried only to go to the toilet when there weren't any soldiers nearby. My fellow prisoners were polite enough not to watch.

Later on, soldiers appeared and called my number. They escorted me from the pen and told me to stop and get undressed. It was winter, and they had a bucket of cold water, which they poured over my head. They enjoyed that. The women stood in a circle around me with their weapons and laughed.

I was ashamed, but I wasn't voluntarily naked. I don't want to repeat what they said, although I remember most of it. They called this treatment the "shower." Some of the other prisoners were also treated this way, and in my case it was usually at the hands of female soldiers. Perhaps it was because, even though I'd lost a lot of weight, I had been in very good shape.

"053, get ready for your shower!"

Ha ha.

Although the water was ice-cold, it felt burning hot on my skin. Sometimes even the water in the bottles that they threw over the fence of our pen was frozen. We could only drink it after we had warmed it up underneath our overalls.

Ha ha.

The prophet Abraham was stripped naked before he was cast into the flames. That's why it is said that he will be the first to receive clothing in paradise. "The help of Allah alone is what I need!" Abraham said when the Archangel Gabriel appeared to offer him his assistance. "God is my protector. I expect help only from him." They threw Abraham into the fire. But he didn't feel the flames, and he wasn't burned. Allah commanded the fire not to burn him, and Abraham felt fine in the flames.

I sat in my usual spot and thought about what would happen next. Two prisoners sat beside me, Erhan and Serkan, or sometimes it was an Arab or an Afghan. We were moved repeatedly. Every couple of days they'd build a new pen, and new prisoners would be brought there. I met some Uzbeks from Afghanistan—their language is like ancient Turkish. There are some eight million people of Turkish descent living in Afghanistan, as I found out; they come from Uzbekistan and Turkmenistan, which border Afghanistan to the north. In Kandahar I began to learn new languages. The Uzbeks also spoke Farsi, and that was helpful because they could help me talk to the Afghans.

"053, get ready!"

I looked around. It was dark.

I went to the fence. A short distance away, next to the Americans, were two other soldiers wearing different uniforms. I noticed that immediately, even in the darkness. I'd never seen uniforms like that in the camp. I studied the uniforms and saw the colors of the German flag on their sleeves. German soldiers? Were these the German soldiers I'd been hoping for? Somehow, I had the feeling that these two soldiers weren't going to get me out of here and take me back home. Still, perhaps it would be possible to send a message back home.

"That's him," said one of the Americans. "That's the German guy."

The German guy. Had the two soldiers come here because of me?

Now I could see them better. They really did have German flags on their epaulettes. One soldier had dark hair; the other was blond and a bit more powerfully built.

I could see their faces. They nodded and looked me in the eye.

"Picked the wrong side, didn't you," said the dark-haired one in German. "Look at the ground!"

That was all they said. They didn't ask me anything, and they didn't seem to want anything from me. I sat back down on my spot.

A half hour later, my number was called again. I lay on my stomach with my hands behind my back, and they put the cuffs on. The escort team led me to a military truck. Behind it were the two German soldiers.

Were they waiting for me? What did they want? Would they help me perhaps?

The escort team threw me to the ground in front of their feet. I heard the Americans step back. The dark-haired soldier approached. He bent down to me and grabbed me by the hair. He pulled my head up and turned it so that we were staring each other in the eye.

"Do you know who we are?" he yelled, again in German. "We're KSK. German special forces."

I didn't say anything. This was not the time for a conversation. I lay there at his feet in the frozen mud, and he held my head in his hands.

Then he slammed my nose into the ground.

The soldier stood up, and I felt a kick. One of the two German soldiers had kicked me in the side. I couldn't see which one it was.

They hadn't come here to help me.

The German soldiers laughed. I heard the escort team, too, begin to laugh a little further off.

Then the Germans went away. They just left me lying there. The escort team came, picked me up and led me back to the pen. I was sitting in my spot again. My head buzzed, I felt nauseous, and my nose was bloody. I asked myself why they had treated me like that. The Americans tortured me because I was supposed to confess to being a terrorist. But why did the Germans do that? Did they hate me for being Turkish?

Still, I hoped that something good would come of the situation. The German soldiers would probably have to file a report. They wouldn't report that they had abused me, but they would mention that they had seen me in the camp. They had to tell the German authorities about me. Then not only my family, but also the state would know that I was being held in an American military base in Kandahar.

That same evening I saw the German special-forces soldiers patrolling the camp with the American troops. As they approached our pen, I could see the blond soldier showing the Americans his machine gun. It was very different from the M-16s the Americans carried. To demonstrate how it worked, the German soldier shouldered his weapon and pointed it at us. I could now see that it was equipped with a laser aiming device. I saw the red dot wander through the gloom, stopping on the heads of the prisoners. The German special forces soldier was only a few meters away from us and was aiming at our heads.

The Americans seemed to be fascinated by this. The dot from the laser went from head to head.

Other soldiers joined their group, expressing their enthusiasm for the weapon.

One day, the first of the prisoners were led away in groups. Word was that they were being moved. But we quickly realized they were being taken away from the camp. But where to? We didn't know. Then someone said they were taking us all away by plane.

They always came and took ten to twenty people. They always took a few people from every group, from every pen. This went on for a couple of weeks. Once a week, the same procedure. The prisoners all had to approach the fence, and those whose numbers were called had to get ready for the escort team. We never saw them again.

The camp was full of rumors. Some people thought they were taking us to a prison in the United States. Others believed we were being set free since they couldn't prove anything against us. Others still thought we were going to the electric chair. For days, we talked about how we were going to die.

"No," said one of the Uzbeks. "In the United States, they inject you with a needle full of poison. You're given some sleeping pills, and when you're unconscious, the poison is injected."

"How do you know?" asked someone else.

"I saw it in an American movie called *Dead Man Walking*. About some guy. In the end he was dead, but he wasn't walking."

We couldn't help but laugh at that.

"No way," said a Pakistani, who claimed to have been in the United States and know the country. "We're going to fry."

"They'll hang us," said the Uzbek. "They still have the death penalty by hanging in the United States."

"They've already hung us," I said and held up my hands.

We kept speculating about how they were going to kill us.

I had been reunited with the two Turks in the same pen, and we could talk with one another.

"But why would they want to torture us to death if we're innocent?" asked Serkan. We asked ourselves what was going to happen next, whether Turks would come and get us and put us in jail.

I had known Erhan and Serkan for some time, but it was only on the final night before we were taken away that I learned where Serkan was from. He said that he had a small carpenter's shop in his hometown. I asked him which town. Sakarya on the Black Sea, he said.

That was where my mother came from.

I had a lot of relatives there, I told him. Every year we went there and spent the summer in a village just outside the main town.

He told me about a certain spot on the sea where I had often gone swimming too. His carpenter's shop was located at a street crossing where an old eucalyptus tree stood. I remembered the street and the tree. Perhaps we had seen one another there on the beach.

I didn't sleep a wink that night. For the first time, I thought again about Turkey, about Sakarya, the town where, a few months previously, I had married Fatima. I thought about my grandfather's village, Kusca. My grandfather grew hazelnut trees there. He made his living from them, just as half of the village had for generations.

I saw the grove in front of his house.

IV

KUSCA, TURKEY

THE VILLAGE OF KUSCA IN THE SAKARYA REGION OF Turkey is surrounded by mountains, but they are full of trees and other lush greenery. The air is warm and soft—it smells like salt and cough drops. Not far from my grandfather's house, the sea rolls in. You can hear the sound of the waves from his yard. A river flows behind his hazelnut grove. I called my grandfather Dédé.

As a child, I used to play every summer amid the trees. When I was hungry, I'd pluck a few nuts from the branches and crack them open. The shells were so soft that I could crack them with my teeth. I'd climb up into the branches and then jump down to the ground. I'd hunt for mice with switches that I carved from the supple branches. But what we liked most was sliding. My cousin Ibrahim and I would often steal metal sheets from my Anane's (Anane is Turkish for grandmother) oven or my mother's, my aunt's, or our neighbors' stoves. Our hazelnut grove sloped steeply toward the river. We'd take the metal sheets, which smelled of baklava and bread, sit on them, and slide down the hill. The sheets were big enough so that we could lie on our stomachs and pick up a head of steam.

Sometimes we'd go tumbling or land in the water. We ate hazelnuts until we were about to burst and our stomachs ached. In Dédé's garden there were also fruit trees, cherries, and apples.

My mother had a sister and two brothers who still lived in the village; we had a big family. I often went swimming with my uncle in the Black Sea. Or sometimes I'd get up on his tractor, and my uncle would let me steer. It was a nice life. We went fishing in the river, using nets instead of poles. We threw back what we'd caught. Anane bought her fish in the village, since it was very cheap.

Sakarya was pure freedom, I thought that night in the prison camp. When we wanted to go fishing, we went fishing. When we wanted to go swimming, we went swimming. Even the cows went swimming, I remembered. The farmers would bring them to the river and herd them in. And when we wanted to go riding, we went riding. We had a horse.

There were animals in the grove, including snakes, some of them poisonous. As long as I didn't frighten the snakes, they wouldn't bite. They would slither over my legs. It would feel raw and cold, and then they'd disappear. I didn't like walking through the brush, though, because I couldn't see where I was stepping. I killed a few snakes out of curiosity, but normally I did them no harm.

One time when Ibrahim and I were older, I saw a very long yellow snake. We had been tramping through the brush on the edge of the grove, and suddenly the snake appeared in front of me. Its skin was glowing yellow, and its belly was white. It was lovely, but it also looked very dangerous. I took a thick branch and bashed it on the head. It rebounded into the air, and I quickly stepped to one side. I hit the snake repeatedly on the head, but it was like the creature was made of rubber. Ibrahim stood there and watched, laughing.

"What are doing?"

"I'm trying to kill the snake. It's dangerous. Come on and help me!"

Ibrahim laughed. He went and got a twig from one of the hazelnut trees and stripped the green bark quickly and skillfully, as if it were a peel, from its hard, white, and very moist interior.

"What are you doing?" I asked. "What good is that little twig?"

Ibrahim grinned. He stood in front of the snake and rubbed it a couple of times gently on the head and belly with the twig. The snake became calm. Then it stopped moving entirely. It was dead.

"How did you do that?" I asked.

"It's like poison for snakes," he said. If I hadn't seen it with my own eyes, I wouldn't have believed it was true.

This was new to me, that strength and aggression aren't always the best answer. I had played with twigs like this as a child and even chewed on a couple of them. The sap didn't hurt me. But for snakes, it was deadly.

———————

I had spent the summer before I was captured in Kusca as well. That was five or six months ago, I thought. It seemed so long ago.

I had announced to my parents that I wanted to get married and start a family. I was old enough to look for a respectable woman. A *multesima*—a Muslim woman who adhered to the rules of Islam.

I had had enough of the girls in Germany. I had had enough of discos and Turks who used and dealt drugs and got sent to prison. And I was sick of my job as a bouncer.

I wanted to do something sensible. I had had both Turkish and German girlfriends. They only lasted a couple of weeks, and sometimes I even had two simultaneously. It was just for fun. I was seventeen or eighteen years old, and I did what all my friends did. Now I wanted to put that behind me.

A *multesima* wouldn't hang around in discos. She wouldn't cheat on me or disappoint me. I could have children with her. But you had to marry a *multesima*, and before I could do that, I had to change my life. I had to become pious and live according to Allah's rules. That's what I did. In the past, I had occasionally drunk alcohol. I put an end to that, and I quit all my jobs as a bouncer.

One day, my aunt called and said she knew a young woman in Kusca I might like. Her parents were religious people. She told me about her and sent a photo.

In Turkish villages, when a young woman reaches a certain age, the family of the young man visits her parents' house and tries to reach an agreement with her family. If the young woman and the young man agree, things can happen very quickly. In our village, there were two large families: mine and Fatima's. My aunt had known Fatima since she was a child. She used to help out around the house.

I called Fatima and we agreed to meet in the summer. We didn't know whether we would like each other. I only had two weeks' vacation because I was about to complete my apprenticeship as a shipbuilder. My whole family drove to Turkey as part of a convoy in my father's Mercedes, as we always did. There were a number of families from Bremen or the surrounding area who were driving to the same region in Turkey or at least in the same direction. Along the way, we would stop and eat together, and other Turkish-German families would join us. At times there were as many as ten cars in the convoy. Turkish people don't like to travel alone. My father took his vacation, and Ali and Alper were on holiday from school. My aunt and uncle were expecting us. I had the time of my life.

My aunt arranged a meeting with Fatima. According to our rules, a man is only allowed to meet with an unmarried woman if a third person is present. It doesn't have to be the parents. The point is that everything stays decent. We met at my aunt's.

When I saw Fatima for the first time, I immediately liked her. I told her about Bremen and how I had grown up. I told her about my apprenticeship, the discos, the kung-fu studio, and I made it clear that I had become a religious person. She and my aunt listened carefully. I told her that I wanted to live with my future wife in Bremen. There was talk that we might marry. Then she told me about herself. At the end of our meeting, I said that I would think things over and that she should do the same—then we could tell one another what we'd decided.

I was already sure after our first meeting that Fatima was the right one for me. I didn't need to meet her a second time. So I asked my parents to start the necessary steps. We don't propose marriage by bending down on one knee in front of the bride-to-be. Our parents make the arrange-ments among themselves, once we have made our decision. My parents delivered my proposal to Fatima's parents. First, in line with our tradi-tion, they had to go shopping. All over Turkey there are stores where you can buy whatever is necessary—everything from a suit to a bridal dress to gifts for the bride's family. One such gift is a special kind of handmade chocolate that isn't meant to be eaten, but rather kept as a memento. My parents drove to a store in Sakarya and bought a watch for Fatima's father, a suit for Fatima's brother, a blouse for her mother, a headscarf, and other such items. Everything was wrapped up nicely. Then my par-ents and my grandmother went to visit Fatima's family with their gifts.

Salam alaikum—Alaikum salam. They had tea. Tradition demanded that I not be present at this meeting. In accordance with custom, my par-ents introduced my proposal, invoking the "command and will of God" and presenting the flowers and gifts, including the chocolate on a silver platter. Fatima's parents then said, also in keeping with tradition, "We'll consider it." Fatima's father knew me, we had met once in the mosque. He remembered me well—but of course he wanted to know what I did for a living and what my future looked like financially. His daughter's wed-ding would be a somewhat sad occasion for him since he wouldn't be see-ing her very often, if she lived in Bremen.

In the end Fatima's father said, "If our children would like to marry, let it bring them happiness." Then he asked Fatima, and she said yes. Everyone shook hands. Then they discussed the details of the wedding. If they hadn't accepted my proposal, Fatima's parents would have given back all the gifts.

Weddings, so people believe in Turkey, always bring good luck. So we spare no expense. It's a question of honor. Every detail of the ceremony is prescribed and follows tradition. One week before the wedding, it was announced via loudspeaker in Kusca and the neighboring villages that Murat Kurnaz was going to marry the daughter of family X (I'd prefer not to give their name) from Kusca. All the inhabitants of the villages were invited.

On the eve of the wedding, the men and the women in our families celebrated separately. The women sang sad songs about Fatima's departure from her childhood home. She wore a red headscarf as a sign of grieving and my mother gave her gold jewelry.

———————

The wedding ceremony took place in my aunt's yard. Hundreds of people came. We sat at a table decorated with flowers, were served like royalty, and got lots of presents. We were given a Koran (a symbol of faith), a candle (a symbol of light), a mirror (a symbol of enlightenment), and rice and sugar—the symbols of fertility and the sweetness of life.

We exchanged rings, bound together with a red ribbon. We were happy. My mother was happy—my father, too, although he had to pay for everything. But he wasn't thinking about money. That is our custom, and many Turks save up for a long time in order to be able to celebrate a wedding some day.

My vacation was coming to an end. Fatima and I had agreed that she would stay with her parents until I had taken care of the formalities in Bremen so that she could emigrate to Germany. That was supposed to be around Christmas. My family stayed in Kusca. I took the bus alone to Istanbul and flew back to Germany.

On the plane, I started to worry. I was now married. I had longed for a wife, and Fatima was a pious *multesima*, just as I had wished. But what did I know about our faith? I had prayed in a few mosques, but the mosques didn't teach us much about Islam. I hardly knew anything about the Koran, about how it had been written and how it was meant to be read. I knew very little about the prophets and the laws and the commandments. How was a pious husband supposed to behave? What were my responsibilities?

I hadn't even really learned to pray properly. For a *multesima*, what I knew wasn't enough. My German friends in Hemelingen had learned about Christianity in school or during communion and confirmation. Religion wasn't taught at my school, and as a child I'd mostly skipped the lessons on Islam at the mosque. I could go back there and sit among six-year-olds in order to catch up but it would take years in Germany until I'd learned everything—there are Islamic schools in Germany, but they are only open on the weekends.

So I thought about what my friends in Bremen had told me about the Jama'at al-Tablighi organization. At mosques in Hemelingen and in the center of Bremen I had heard about the Masura Center in Lahore. There I'd be able to learn everything I needed to know in order to be a good husband and a good Muslim in less than two months. That's how I imagined it on the plane back to Germany.

A stewardess came and asked me if I wanted something to drink. I didn't look at her. That much I already knew: If I was going to be a good Muslim, I was no longer allowed to look at another woman. We refrain from doing this not out of a lack of respect for women, but because we hold them in such high regard. I looked at the floor of the plane and ordered a Coke.

I had thought about going to Pakistan and studying at the Mansura Center for some time; now my mind was finally made up. I could go there and be back by Christmas. It was my last chance, and my last adventure, before Fatima came to Germany.

V

GUANTANAMO BAY, CAMP X-RAY

"053, GET READY FOR THE ESCORT TEAM!"

It was still dark. The numbers of Erhan and Serkan and of the two Uzbeks were also called. It was our turn.

We were gathered at a spot in front of the open hanger, led off one by one, and brought to a tent. There they cut off our beards and shaved our heads. At least they would no longer be able to drag me around by the hair, I thought.

We received new orange-colored overalls, and they chained us back up.

"We're gonna put you now into the same cave with Osama bin Laden," said the soldier who had shaved my head, "and then we're gonna shoot you."

They didn't put a sack over my head this time. Instead they wrapped it up like a package with soundproof headphones, a gas mask, blinders, and watertight, thick black diving goggles. The soldier tightened the handcuffs so that they immediately began to hurt. It was hardly bearable.

"Too strong," I murmured underneath the mask. I was trying to tell the soldier that the handcuffs were too tight, but I didn't know the right word.

"Let me see," I heard another soldier say, who must have been standing next to the first one. I held out the cuffs in his direction, but he tightened them even more around my wrists. You bastard, I thought. He put something thick and stiff over my hands—gloves or maybe mittens. Then he hit me in the face and kicked me in the genitals. I fell. They carried me out of the tent and threw me on the ground. I was told to lie there on my side.

"You guys are going to get shot," the soldier said.

That I understood. And as I lay there for four, five, or maybe six hours in front of the hangar, I also understood the purpose of all of the get-up. The gloves weren't meant to warm my hands, and the headphones and mask weren't there to protect my ears and face. They were there to ensure the soldiers' safety, so we couldn't bite, scratch, or spit at them. We couldn't cough any bacteria into their faces, spread any germs, or infect them with a disease. They didn't care whether we suffocated under the masks.

I knew what awaited us: a first-class flight. They chained us together and herded us onto the plane. We were bound so tightly we couldn't move a millimeter. Again, I thought that they were taking us to an American military base in Turkey. What else was I supposed to think?

Sleep would have been the only consolation in such a situation. But the soldiers kept hitting us to keep us awake. I thought about the American movies I had seen in Bremen. Action flicks and war movies. I used to admire the Americans. Now I was getting to know their true nature.

I say that without anger. It's simply the truth, as I saw and experienced it. I don't want to insult anyone, and I'm not talking about all Americans. But the ones I encountered are terrified of pain. They're afraid of every little scratch, bacteria, and illness. They're like little girls, I'd say. If you examine Americans closely, you realize this—no matter how big or powerful they are. But in movies, they're always the heroes.

The flight must have lasted twenty-seven hours. Somewhere we made a stopover. We weren't able to move throughout the entire flight. They never loosened the restraints, not for a moment. We didn't know where we had landed or where they were taking us. We didn't even know if we were going to arrive alive.

———————

I felt the heat immediately and could hear the barking of dogs in spite of the soundproof headphones. Through the goggles, I could perceive the bright light of the sun. On the runway, the first prisoners collapsed. They took off our face masks. The sunlight was blinding. We were told to lie on the ground. I kept my eyes closed. I heard the clicking of cameras. We were being photographed.

"Don't move."

I carefully opened my eyes, but all I could see were boots on the glittering concrete surface. They put our masks back on—mine was a bit loose. They herded us into a bus. It was white. It was dark inside the vehicle. There were no seats in the bus, just hooks attached to the floor. They chained us to the hooks so that we could neither sit nor stand properly. They kept hitting us, and the dogs, which had been taken onto bus, bit us.

"Don't sit like that!"

A blow followed.

"Sit differently!"

Another blow.

"Sit up straight!"

It was unbelievably hot on the bus. We must be in a country with warm winters, I thought. Southern Turkey? It was February or March. Maybe somewhere near the city of Adana. Adana could have been this hot. It was definitely above ninety degrees.

I felt the bus drive across a bridge or an on-ramp. Then we stopped. The bus began to sway. We must be on a ship, I thought. They were kicking us constantly, and the ship listed to one side. Is there an American military base on an island off the coast of Adana, I asked myself. Or are they taking us to Cyprus? Then we rolled back down the ramp and left the ship. At some point—we couldn't have driven more than a half-hour—the bus stopped.

"Get out! Out!"

We had to kneel and lower our heads to our chests. There was a crunching sound. From under my mask, I could see gravel. I don't know how long exactly we knelt there. Several hours. The heat was unbearable. In Afghanistan and on the plane, it had been ice-cold. The soldiers were constantly yelling and hitting us. At last, I was allowed to stand up. The soldiers pushed me forward, and I stumbled barefoot across the gravel. The way was long, with lots of left and right turns. They yelled at me the whole time.

"Terrorist!"

"We'll kill you!"

"Motherfucker!"

Then a soldier yelled, "Stop!" Someone took the mask from my head. I was standing in a tent. I saw a name tag. It was the first time I saw a soldier with his name on his chest. I will never forget it. Two other soldiers held my arms tight. They took off the gloves.

"I speak German," said the man with the name tag. "We're going to have a really great time together."

A number of soldiers were busy doing things to me. They pulled out hairs from my arms, put a swab in my mouth, and took my fingerprints. Someone was always fiddling with me. The procedure took quite a while. I kept looking at the one soldier's chest, at his name tag. I was weighed, and they measured my height.

"Name?" they asked.

Murat Kurnaz.

Spelling!

K-U-R-N-A-Z.

It was a wonder to me that I could still talk. I hadn't slept properly in weeks because of the noise from the planes, bombs, and electrical generators in Kandahar and because of the interrogations. But at least I was standing up. I was happy to be standing because we sat the whole time on the plane. I didn't know how I was able to stand. It was almost as though the name tag on the male soldier's chest was keeping me upright. I will call him Cecil Stewart.

They put an armband on me. There was a new number on it: 061. It was green and made of plastic.

"This is a nice place," said one of the soldiers who had taken hair and saliva samples. "Lots of trees."

Trees? Were they making fun of me?

He pointed outside the tent.

The tent door was open. I couldn't see any trees. I saw hills. Hills and sand and cactus. Big cactus. There aren't any trees where cacti grow.

"Do you know why you're here?" I heard the man with the nametag ask.

"Do you know what the Germans did to the Jews?" he said. "That's exactly what we're going to do with you."

Someone grabbed me by the shirt and pushed me out of the tent. Outside I saw a number of tightly packed rows of chain-link fence. It was like a labyrinth. I saw another prisoner in his orange overalls being led through the fencing. The soldiers immediately threw me to the ground. I landed on the gravel. "Lie there!" The man with the nametag pressed his knee into the back of my neck, pushing my face into the gravel, so that I could no longer see the other prisoner and the escort team. Only when they were out of sight did we move on.

Where is the prison they're taking me to? I asked myself.

We passed through a number of doors in the chain-link fence and arrived at a pen, also made of chain-link fence. These were cages. Prisoners in orange overalls were already sitting there, each in their own little cages. One beside the other, all in a row, like tigers or lions in a zoo. The labyrinth had to be pretty big if we were all going to fit in here. Surely these strange cages were only an intermediate station. But all I could see around me were hills and cactus. Maybe the prison was over the crest of one of the hills. The soldiers opened up a cage and pushed me inside. I was told to kneel.

"You are Charlie-Charlie-3. Say it!"

"Charlie-Charlie-3," I said. I had trouble understanding. Why was my cage called Charlie-Charlie-3?

Then the soldier took off the chains and locked the door in the fence.

"Sit down!" they ordered.

I sat down.

"Don't move!" they snarled.

I didn't move. They yelled something else that I didn't understand, but I suspected it was about how they were going to kill me. But surely they could have done that a lot more easily earlier. The soldiers left.

I thought they would come back in a few minutes and get me. I sat somewhat more comfortably Indian-style and collected myself. I rubbed my wrists and ankles, which were swollen and bloody. At least they had taken the cuffs off. That felt better, and I calmed down a bit, even though I felt a stinging sensation, as if being poked by a thousand needles. I need to distract myself so I looked around.

In the cage, there were two plastic buckets, the color of eggshells and semitransparent. One contained some water that stank. Perhaps for washing, I thought. The other seemed to be the toilet. There was a thin foam mattress, less than an inch thick, on the ground and a blanket on top. Next to the blanket were a piece of soap, a towel, and a pair of flip-flops. We'll be taking these new things with us, I thought. We're probably just waiting here while they prepare our cells.

The prisoners in the other cages greeted me.

Salam alaikum.

Alaikum salam.

One of the prisoners in a nearby cage looked like an Afghan Uzbek. He, too, greeted me. I asked him in Turkish how long he'd been here, but he didn't understand. I tried to communicate with my hands. You? Here? I counted on my fingers: one, two, three, four . . .

The Uzbek answered in his native tongue and held up all his fingers twice: "Twenty." I took this to mean twenty minutes. He'd been in his cage twenty minutes longer than I had in mine.

I waited. Someone would soon come and get us. Still seated, I measured my cage with my hand. I knew from my shipbuilder's apprenticeship how long the span between my thumb and little finger was when my fingers were stretched out. So I didn't need a measuring tape to figure out that the cage was six feet by seven. It was around six feet high. All told, it was less than fifteen square feet. In Germany, there's a law that kennels in the animal shelter have to be at least twenty square feet. I knew that because I myself had been a dog owner.

I waited and looked around. Not far from me, a prisoner was being led through the chain-link fences. He was still wearing his mask and the soundproof headphones, and I heard the soldiers screaming at him. They kept walking back and forth along the same passageway. Now I understood how we had come here. I thought that we had walked a long distance, but the spot where we had been forced to kneel for hours before they took the mask off was only a few yards away from my cage. We had kneeled directly beside one another, but we didn't know that. They led us around in circles until we thought that we were in a large camp or a prison. But the whole time we had always been in the same place within the maze of chain-link fence pens.

I thought, if it's March, my birthday is coming up. What a surprise.

Suddenly I heard a quiet splashing. A frog was swimming in the bucket of water. I had only ever seen them on television—frogs don't live on the Weser River in Bremen. It must have been looking for water in this desert. Where had it come from? I fished him out of the stinking water. It sat on my hand and looked at me, breathing rapidly. I tried to pat it gently, but it hopped to the ground and disappeared through the fence.

Hour upon hour I waited. No one came. No one was brought away and relocated. In the end, guards came with something to eat. On paper plates, as I saw from a distance, but it was something. Until now we had only ever gotten Emaries. I was looking forward to eating some real food. Maybe everything would get better. It couldn't be any worse than in Kandahar.

That would prove to be a mistake . . . in every respect.

As the guards approached my cage, all I saw on the plate were three spoonfuls of rice, a slice of dry bread, and a plastic spoon. That was it.

They shoved the plates through a small square opening around knee-height within the fencing. I thought there must be some sort of mistake. Perhaps something had fallen off the plate. Then I saw the rations given to the Uzbek. It was the same miserably tiny pile of rice, or maybe even less. I would have rather had an Emarie. At least they contained crackers.

I ate the rice and looked at my armband. The rice was cold and not fully cooked; the kernels were as hard as sand. But it was all I had to eat. My armband read: "Kunn, Murat, male, Turkish, 5-foot-4, 165 pounds."

They had misspelled my name—after all the time they kept me in custody and despite having confiscated my travel papers. I drank some water from the bucket. I was exhausted. The difference in climate between here and Kandahar was enormous.

Suddenly, within a matter of minutes, the sky grew dark. The sun was gone, and harsh bright lights were switched on. The light came from neon lamps affixed to the corrugated aluminum roof and a large number of spotlights that were mounted on sentry posts and the fences. It reminded me of the soccer stadium in Bremen. From loudspeakers that must have been hanging somewhere, there came some static and then a call to prayer. The time for evening prayers was a while ago, I thought, but then suddenly the voice was drowned out by loud music. It was the American national anthem. I heard the other prisoners start to complain, but that didn't help. At some point, I knelt, carried out the prayer ritual and said as well as I could in Arabic: "Praise be to Allah. Allah hears all who praise him." I bowed thirty-three times. Rock music was now blaring from the speakers, almost too loud to bear. The volume was louder than in any Bremen disco I'd ever experienced.

I had a sneaking suspicion that the Uzbek hadn't been saying he'd been in his cage twenty minutes longer than me. He had meant twenty days. They weren't going to be taking us to prison today. That was all right by me. Despite the light and the noise, all I wanted to do was sleep.

But I couldn't sleep. Every few minutes, guards came and pounded the fence with their nightsticks. Every few minutes someone, sometimes next to me and sometimes in front of me, killed something in his cage and threw it out—snakes, rats, and spiders. The guards' boots crunched on the gravel. And then there were the 1,000-watt spotlights.

The guards returned. We all had to get up and "identify ourselves." We had to extend our hands through the opening in the cage where the food had been shoved through, so that they could read our armbands. Later they pounded on the fencing of my cage because I had my hands under the blanket.

"Take your hands out!"

Later still, they rattled the fencing because I was lying on my side.

"Lie on your back!"

At some point, I feel asleep from sheer exhaustion.

Camp X-Ray had been built especially for us, and true to its name, it was supposed to be a prison camp in which everything was completely transparent. This was something entirely new. There were no cells where you could be alone. There was no privacy, no protection from the watching eyes of the guards or the cameras, not even for a second. The cages were so small that it drove you to desperation. At the same time, nature—and freedom—were so tantalizingly close it could make you go crazy. An animal has more space in its cage in a zoo and is given more to eat. I can hardly put into words what that actually means.

The cellblocks all had a second roof of corrugated tin, but the cages were still somewhat in the wilderness. The sun beat down, and there was no refuge in the shade unless the sun was shining directly on the tin roof, which hung about a foot above the chain-link fence roof proper of the cages. The aluminum also heated up fast. We were just as exposed to the rain since it always was driven in from the side. You couldn't escape it no matter which corner of the cage you crept into.

The camp contained six cell-blocks: Alpha, Bravo, Charlie, Delta, Echo, and Foxtrot. The blocks were separated by narrow corridors through the chain-link fence pens. Every block had six wings, also named from Alpha to Foxtrot. A wing consisted of ten cages arranged at a right angle. Every cage had a name: Alpha-Bravo 1, Bravo-Charlie 5, Delta-Alpha 9. I was in Charlie-Charlie 3. There were high chain-link walls around the six blocks, interrupted by guard towers with sharp-shooters.

The initial days in Camp X-Ray weren't easy. I didn't know we were in Cuba. I had no idea what rules applied here. The rules were constantly changing anyway, and you'd get punished for breaking them. The first night I learned that I was only allowed to cover my legs, and nothing else, with the blanket, and that I wasn't allowed to sleep on my side, only on my back. In the days that followed, I learned that I wasn't allowed to get up and walk around my cage. During the day, we had to remain seated and at night we had to lie down. If you lay down during the day, you were punished. We weren't allowed to touch the fence or even lean our backs up against it. We weren't allowed to talk. We weren't to speak to or look at the guards. We weren't allowed to draw in the sand or whistle or sing or smile. Every time I unknowingly broke a rule or, because they had just invented a new one, did something I shouldn't have, the IRF team would come and beat me.

IRF stood for "Immediate Reaction Force" and consisted of five to eight soldiers with plastic shields, breastplates, hard-plastic knee-, elbow-, and shoulder-protectors, helmets with plastic visors, gloves with hard-plastic knuckles, heavy boots, and billy clubs. I would say they were thugs. Thugs whose entire bodies were protected by bullet- and knife-proof gear. They didn't have weapons with them other than the billy clubs—probably because they were afraid of us getting our hands on them.

I often saw fear in their eyes as they stood in front of our cages and waited to be deployed, even though we didn't have shoes on and were already cowering on the ground. They came with pepper spray in a kind of pressurized aerosol gun that they could aim precisely at a prisoner from ten feet away. It contained oleoresin capisicum, which is made from chili peppers. They sprayed the entire cage and waited until the prisoner was completely unable to resist. Then they stormed in.

"Get up!"

"Hurry!"

"Get up!"

I heard loud rock music, and I heard their commands. The pepper spray burned my nose, throat, and eyes. I had to cough. The burning was diabolical.

"Get up!" they yelled.

"Get to the wall!"

"Hands to the wall!"

"Move! Move!"

I couldn't see anything, couldn't breathe, and didn't know what was happening to me. I heard them beating the fence with their billy clubs. When the cage door was opened, I heard them yelling. I felt a baton blow to my head. I huddled, and they beat me. They picked me up and threw me to the ground. They kicked and punched me. I curled up into a ball. Then I got angry and tried to defend myself. I jumped to my feet, blind, and started swinging my arms. I got hold of someone's helmet, but they forced me back down and grabbed me by the genitals. They held my arms and legs to the ground, until I was lying there like an animal about to be drawn and quartered. One of them pressed his shield on my chest, while another punched me in the face. At some point, I couldn't hear the music anymore. I heard nothing.

I didn't get much sleep the night of my first visit from the IRF team. I lay on my back—shaken by throbbing pain and the pounding bass from the music—and tried not to move. I had learned that I was only allowed to cover my legs with the blanket and had to keep my hands in plain view on my stomach. I heard the IRF team many times that night. I prayed to Allah that they wouldn't return to my cage.

The next morning, my whole body hurt. I sat up and looked around. It was still dark outside the fences, but breakfast had already arrived: a hard-boiled egg without its shell, a slice of dry bread, and a few peas. I heard a couple of the prisoners calling to the guards. It was always the same word:

"Tee-pee!"

A short time later, the guards came and brought the prisoners a small piece of toilet paper. They shoved through the square hole in the cage.

"TP!" I called.

"TP?"

I didn't get any toilet paper. I had learned that toilet paper was a matter left entirely up to the guard. If he felt like giving you some, you got some. If not, you had to improvise.

A short time later, the escort team arrived. They bound me, and we walked through the corridors in the chain-link fencing. They pressed my head down so that I couldn't look around. At every door, the guard who did the unlocking read my armband and searched me for weapons. We left Block Charlie, went through the corridor between Charlie and Bravo, walked along Bravo and arrived in the corridor between Bravo and Alpha. All I could see was the gravel and the cages with other prisoners. Suddenly someone called out in Turkish.

"Murat, Murat! It's me!"

It was Nuri's voice.

Nuri was a Turk I'd met in Kandahar. He sat next to me in front of the hangar while we were waiting to be loaded on to the plane. He had looked terrible. His eyes were swollen, his lips were split, his wrists and ankles bled from the cuffs, and some of his teeth had been knocked out. I had asked him what his name was and where he came from. He said he came from Izmir. That was the city where my father was born.

Nuri was an electrician. He was married and had two children. We had heard the constant screaming of prisoners being tortured in the hangar. Nuri had said:

"Now we're going back to where we came from."

Allah, he said, had created us from earth, and the earth was where we would return.

"Do you think," Nuri had asked, "that they'll just let us go after all they've done to us?"

"In any case, it will be better than here," I had answered, "whether or not they kill us."

Nuri had laughed. "You're right. But I'm still worried about my children."

———————

So Nuri was here. I heard him, but I wasn't able to turn my head enough to see him. I couldn't answer.

"Try to get transferred to Block Alpha."

How was I supposed to do that?

"Ask the guards," he said. "Ask them to move you here."

I heard him call the guards. They stopped and let my head go. Nuri glared at one of them and gestured for him to come closer. He pointed to an insect crawling on his arm. He pointed to the guard, as though saying: You are this insect. Then he squashed the bug with his hand.

We came to an open space. There was an electric car like a golf cart. We drove in it past a row of long, low buildings, made of chipboard. They were arranged in blocks of four, raised on stilts about three feet off the ground.

Soldiers and an African American woman in uniform waited in front of the building where we stopped. The soldiers frisked me, then the woman asked:

"Do you have any weapons?"

That was ridiculous. Where was I supposed to get any weapons?

I said, "Yes, I have."

"Where?" the woman asked and immediately took a step back.

I bared my teeth.

The woman ran away, calling out that I had tried to bite her. Other soldiers hurried up and threw me on the ground.

"You want to bite the guards?"

One spoke loudly and quickly. I could hardly understand a word.

"No, no," I said. "No problem. I don't bite women."

They pressed me to the ground and screamed at me. They were nervous. I hadn't been counting on that. I heard them call an IRF team.

"He wants to bite," the officer said.

The IRF team hit me a couple of times. Then they picked me up and brought me into one of the wooden buildings. There were two rooms, fifteen to twenty square feet, obviously for interrogations. The building had looked much bigger from the outside. There was a chair in the middle of the room. I was told to sit. There was a massive ring in the floor, and they attached the chains between my feet to it with a padlock. The chains around my feet were attached to another chain that ran around my stomach and was attached to my handcuffs.

I couldn't stand up, raise my hands, or even move. In front of me was a table and another chair. That was all. There were two doors but no windows. All around me there was compressed wood. Even the table was made of compressed wood. I looked around the bare space. I didn't see a camera or a mirror. My interrogator would enter through the second door. Behind it there had to be another room, the camera room. But where were the cameras? A guard stood at my side.

My interrogator came out of the second door. He was in his mid-forties.

"This is a great opportunity," he said in German. "I'm looking forward to speaking German with you. I don't want to forget it."

He spoke with an accent, but his German was fluent. I was surprised. At least I would have the chance to explain myself in German and prove my innocence. But before I could say a word, he told me that he went to university for a few years in Germany. I think he said in Frankfurt. I waited for him to finish.

He lit a cigarette.

He didn't ask me any questions. Instead, he just talked. He had shared a house with other American students, and they had regularly smoked hashish. A woman from the authorities regularly came to their house with a dog trained to sniff out drugs. But they knew when she was coming so they would break the hashish into little pieces and spread it all over the carpet with a toothbrush. The dog went crazy because he smelled the scent of hashish everywhere, and the woman was happy because she seemed to have discovered the drugs. But she couldn't find them, and every time she left disappointed.

Why was he telling me this silly story?

He was excitable. A lot of the time, he was laughing. There was a file with some papers and a pen on his desk. He told me some more stories, which bored me. He was talking as if I were hardly even there. I think all he wanted was to hear himself speaking German. Or was he trying to win me over?

Whatever, I thought. At least, I was sitting in a chair and no one was beating me.

Suddenly he asked: "Do you know what we have in store for you?"

I smiled and held the smile long enough so he was sure to see it.

"Yes," I said.

His expression changed. He had probably been expecting a different reaction. He continued to smoke.

I had hoped I would finally be allowed to explain. But I soon realized that this man wasn't at all interested in whether or not I was innocent.

"Tell me your life story," he said.

I started telling him about my apprenticeship as a shipbuilder.

"No, start with your childhood," he said. "Tell me about your childhood."

I told him about going to school in Hemelingen, but he kept interrupting me, he wanted to know names. The names of the friends I had mentioned. He wanted to know if I had any girlfriends—their names interested him, too. He wanted to know when and where I had spent my time and which discotheques I had worked for. Names, names, names.

He said it was obvious that as a terrorist I had only tried to hide in the discos, that I was using them for cover.

"I know you terrorists," he said.

Why should I have tried to hide in a disco?

"You didn't use to wear a beard," he said. "A disguise. You only used your girlfriends."

He was always interrupting me. Did he really think I was a major terrorist?

"I know all your stories. You might as well start with the truth."

He kept smoking.

I told him about my interest in kung-fu.

"Typical for terrorists," he said. "You've all had training in martial arts. Of course, you have. But you're probably the only one who admits it."

He wanted to know which fitness and karate studios I'd worked out in. He said he himself went to a fitness studio.

"Mohammed Atta had a fitness studio in Germany, but behind the scenes he planned his attacks. Just like you."

"I only worked out in my studio in Bremen, nothing else," I said. "I don't know what Mohammed Atta did. I only know him from television."

He wrote down everything I said. I noticed that he used a different pen than the one he had put on the table at the beginning of the interrogation, which he had handled so strangely. It dawned on me that there had to be a hidden camera in that pen. He had placed it on the desk with the cover pointing directly at me so that the camera could film me head on. He never used it for writing, and he handled it so carefully that I knew it had to contain a miniature camera. That much I knew about electronics.

The interrogation lasted for several hours. I told him everything up to the day of my arrest in Peshawar. A few times he stood up and left the room briefly. Perhaps he went to get a bite to eat or something to drink.

He packed up his files and carefully put the camera-pen into his breast pocket.

"That's enough for today," he said. "I know you're lying. From the beginning to the end. That's only going to make your situation worse. Bad luck, boy. You shouldn't lie."

"I'm not lying. Why should I be lying?"

"We know exactly who you are. But we wanted to hear it from you in your own words. You blew your chance!"

Then he left, and the escort team brought me back to my cage. They searched me for weapons and then left me alone.

In the meantime, my sneaking suspicion had become a certainty. The Uzbek had indeed meant twenty days and not twenty minutes. The cages weren't temporary pens. They *were* the prison, wherever it was we were. There wasn't going to be anything else. These cages were my future. I realized that now. But for how long? *Chayr Insha Allah.* With Allah's will, good things should happen.

But how could any good things happen here?

The guards came and said: "Get ready for a shower!"

I remembered those words from Kandahar.

I stripped down to the boxer shorts they had given us, put the towel, soap, and flip-flops under my arm and waited. They came back with the IRF team and a German shepherd. What had I done wrong now? I only learned later that some prisoners were always accompanied by the IRF team when they were taken to showers or interrogations. They were the ones who were especially strong or had trained in martial arts. Others were just escorted by normal guards.

"Turn around and get on your knees! Hands on your head!"

I turned around, knelt, and put my hands on my head. They entered the cage and put me in handcuffs and foot shackles. Then we walked through the chain-link fences until we got to the showers. They were ordinary cages like the ones in which we were imprisoned, but they were divided in two and there was a hose hanging from the fence. A guard outside the cage turned on the water. They put me in the cage and took off the handcuffs. A thin stream of water came out of the hose. I stepped under it, and as I took the soap and lathered myself up, a quick countdown began. Three-two-one-over. There was no more water. My body was still covered in soap suds, but the soldier operating the tap said:

"Your time is up."

That was what they called taking a shower.

On the way back to my cage, one of the soldiers asked me if I worked out and, if so, in what form.

"Hey, you got big arms," he said. "What do you do?"

I said nothing.

When I arrived back at my cage, I could hardly believe my eyes. There was a new prisoner in Charlie-Charlie 1, which had previously been unoccupied. He was young, around my age, maybe nineteen or twenty. He lay on the ground, making soft noises. He wasn't crying. Instead I thought I could make out something of a melody, a sad song in Arabic. He didn't have any legs. His wounds were still fresh.

I sat in my cage, hardly daring to look, but every once in a while I had to glance in his direction. The stumps of his legs were full of pus. The bandages wrapped around them had turned red and yellow. Everything was bloody and moist. He had frostbite marks on his hands. He seemed hardly able to move his fingers. I watched as he tried to get up. He crawled over to the bucket in his cage and tried to sit on it. He had to go to the toilet. He tried to raise himself up with his hands on the chain-link fence, but he didn't make it. He couldn't hold on with his swollen fingers. Still he tried, until a guard came and hit his hands with his billy-club. The young man fell to the ground.

Every time he tried to hoist himself onto the bucket, the guards came and hit him on the hands. No one was allowed to touch the fence—that was an iron law. But a young man with no legs? They told him he wasn't allowed to stand up. But how could he have done that without any legs? He wasn't even allowed to lean on the fence or to crawl onto the bucket.

Over the next few days, I talked to him a bit. I could hardly understand him. His name was Abdul Rahman, and he came from Saudi Arabia. I think he said he had been at Bagram, where he had been exposed to extreme cold, just as we had at Kandahar. That's why he had frostbite in his fingers and legs. American doctors had amputated his legs at a military field hospital.

I felt incredibly sorry for Abdul. He must have been in unbelievable pain, and he looked half-starved to death. Nonetheless, they just threw him in a cage and left him lying there instead of treating his injuries. How was he supposed to survive? What kind of doctors were they? And the guards that hit his hands . . . what kind of people were they?

The bandages wrapped around Abdul's stumps were never changed. When he took them off himself, they were full of blood and pus. He showed the bandage to the guards and pointed to his open wounds. The guards ignored him. Later I saw how he tried to wash the bandages in his bucket of drinking water. But he could hardly move his hands, so he wasn't able to. And even if he had, where would he have hung them up to dry? He wasn't allowed to touch the fence. He wrapped his stumps back up in the dirty bandages.

When the guards came to take him to be interrogated, they ordered him to sit with his back to the door and put his hands on his head. When they opened the door, they stormed in as they did with every other prisoner. They hit him on the back and pushed him on the ground. Then they handcuffed and bound him so he could no longer move. Abdul howled in pain.

Why did they do this? He had no legs and only weighed around a hundred pounds. What could he do to them? Abdul was carried to interrogation. The guards put their arms under his armpits, pressing his shoulders, neck, and head down. They lifted him and carried him through the corridor, his stumps dangling in the air. Abdul cried out horribly. When he was brought back hours later, his face always looked like he had been beaten.

We spent a few weeks together in Charlie-Charlie. Abdul was always friendly and pleasant, a real nice guy. It took a while for us to communicate, but in the end we managed. I learned that, like myself, he was newly married. His wedding had been a couple of months ago. I asked him if his wife knew he had lost his legs. Of course she didn't—I should have known better. No one knew anything about us. We talked about sports a lot. Abdul said he liked playing soccer.

The strange thing was how calm he remained, even though he was in terrible pain. He was a person who never lost interest in others despite his own atrocious situation. When the IRF team beat him, he never cried. But when he heard or saw them beating prisoners in the other cages, he did cry. He cried in a loud voice. He still felt sympathy for others, even though he himself had been treated so inhumanely. Then he was moved, and I never saw him again.

Today I know that Abdul survived his injuries. His wounds healed, and he can use his hands again. He's gained weight, and he tries to keep himself in shape. I've heard from another prisoner that he can even do push-ups. Abdul had told the other inmate to say hi to me. As of 2007, he's still being held captive at Guantanamo.

Abdul wasn't the only prisoner who had parts of his body amputated. I saw other such cases in Guantanamo. I know of a prisoner who complained of a toothache. He was brought to a dentist, who pulled out his healthy teeth as well as the rotten one. I knew a man from Morocco who used to be a ship captain. He couldn't move one of his little fingers because of frostbite. The rest of his fingers were all right. They told him they would amputate the little finger. They brought him to the doctor, and when he came back, he had no fingers left. They had amputated everything but his thumbs.

A lot of Afghans had been injured or maimed in the fighting. Some of them were missing an arm or a leg. I saw open wounds that weren't treated. A lot of people had been beaten so often they had broken legs, arms, and feet. The fractures, too, remained untreated. In Camp X-Ray I saw a man taken away to interrogation. When he returned, his arm was dangling as though it was only attached to the rest of his body by skin and tissue. The bone in his arm must have been completely severed, but he was simply thrown back into his cage. How was it supposed to heal?

I never saw anyone in a cast. That will heal by itself, the guards always said. Shortly before my release, I met another prisoner who had had two of his fingers broken by the IRF team. The swelling got worse over the days and weeks. I saw some of the people who suffered these injuries again. Others simply disappeared. Or perhaps I didn't recognize them. In the initial days in Camp X-Ray, we all had shaved heads and faces. Later most of us had long beards and hair. There were always prisoners whose arms, legs, and fingers had healed crookedly. They couldn't use their fingers or their limbs. Some of them only had one arm.

Over the years, I had a lot of toothaches and other health problems. But I tried to avoid being taken to the doctor at all costs. I wanted to keep my teeth, fingers, and legs.

I saw an elderly man who was blind. He was interrogated, beaten, and tortured the same way the rest of us were. The Americans didn't distinguish among us. The man, I was told, was over ninety. He was an Afghan. His hair and his beard were as white as snow.

A prisoner in a cage next to mine at Camp X-Ray told me his father was also being held at Guantanamo. He had asked the guards a number of times to be allowed to see him. They refused. It was not a unique case. There were lots of fathers and sons in Guantanamo. I knew an eighteen-year-old whose fifty-year-old father was also being kept prisoner. There were also lots of brothers. The fathers had to watch as their sons were beaten, and vice versa. Who can stand to watch his own father being beaten up? In Camp Delta, I saw the IRF team mistreat a prisoner in the cage facing mine. His son was imprisoned next to me. He was forced to watch everything.

Once in Camp X-Ray, I spit at a guard who had hit the old man. They came and said, You're going to be punished! I answered, What are you going to do, lock me up? I'm already in this cage. They beat me up. I'm not proud of what I did, but with some people all you can do is spit on them. This particular guard was maybe twenty or twenty-five years old. The old man was blind. I'd never experienced anything like it. How can people be so awful, so repulsive?

The first time I saw Abdul, I thanked my God that he had spared me that fate. I thanked Allah that I was doing a lot better than Abdul, although I was being tortured and kept locked up in a cage. Sometimes, when I heard the IRF team coming to Charlie-Charlie, I prayed they would come and beat me up and not Abdul.

During one of my interrogations, the American who spoke German showed me some newspaper clippings. They'd been printed out from a computer, and you could see the logo of the newspaper. The *New York Times*, the *Washington Post*. There was a whole pile of them. He translated the headlines.

"German Taliban Captured by Special Forces in Afghanistan Fighting."

Had they written those articles themselves? They sounded genuine. My interrogator read a couple of paragraphs out loud in English, then he translated: "Units of American special forces succeeded in capturing a German Taliban during fighting in the mountains of Afghanistan. The man who was trained in martial arts put up bitter resistance . . ."

An American newspaper had written such lies about me?

"But you know that I was captured in Pakistan," I said.

"Yes, we know it," the man answered. "But the people on the outside don't know it. It's none of our business. Journalists write whatever they want."

The American laughed.

At night the creatures came. Perhaps they came down from the hills I could see during the day. Our cages were full of spiders, black widows, and small tarantulas. The tarantulas were black and covered in thick fur. We became good friends. The guards had no objection to us being visited by spiders. Family visits weren't allowed, but spiders were. I didn't care. Tarantulas don't kill people. If they bite you, all you get is a headache. The guards used to crush them into the gravel under their boots.

There was another type of spider the guards were afraid of. They called it the "brown la cruz" or something like that. The spider was reddish-brown, very small, and, with the exception of its backside, hairless. It was supposedly far more poisonous than a tarantula. Its bite could be fatal if not treated immediately. The spiders were able to jump. I always caught them and threw them as far away as I could. I didn't kill them. They hadn't done anything to me. You shouldn't kill any animal you don't intend to eat. The same goes for plants. Snakes also came at night. They were attracted by the warmth of the gravel and concrete.

Charlie-Charlie was one of the outer rows of cages so we were the nearest to the surrounding natural environment. I never got as many visitors as I did there. One time a boa constrictor came. It was very long and thin, and I thought—it still has a lot of growing to do. There were various kinds of snakes, brown ones, green, gray. But they did us no harm. I remembered the snakes in my grandfather's yard and in the hazelnut grove. I thought about the yellow one I had tried to kill with a branch and which Ibrahim had taken care of with a hazelnut twig. Now I felt sorry for it.

One night, I had just fallen asleep despite the din from the loudspeakers, when I felt something crawling on my hand. It felt like someone was trying to tickle me. I thought in my half-sleep that I was at home and my mother was trying to wake me up. She often used to wake me up by tickling me. I opened my eyes and saw that there was a scorpion on my hand. A little black scorpion. I threw it to the ground and crushed it under my foot. I knew that if I did this quickly he wouldn't have time to sting my foot.

Frogs often slipped through the chain-link fence. They looked nice. I don't know how they got into my cage, but suddenly they'd be sitting there. They were in search of water and would leap into the bucket. Sometimes I only saw them when I was drinking. They would be crouching at the bottom of the bucket. That always cheered me up.

The animals I liked best were the iguanas. I always kept some of my slice of bread to feed them. I rolled up the bread into tiny balls and scattered it in front of them on the ground. The iguanas had various colors, green, greenish yellow, or gray. They looked like tiny dragons. Some of them were too big to slip into the cage. But they came anyway. I would flick breadcrumbs through the chain link. They got used to it.

Iguanas? Where were we?

Hummingbirds also visited me in my cage. I had read a lot about hummingbirds. Weren't they native to the Caribbean?

Some time later I heard another prisoner say he thought we might be in Cuba. One of them said the Americans had a military base in Cuba. So I asked one of the interrogators, We're in Cuba, aren't we?

Yes, he said, we're in Cuba.

The cage next to me had become vacant. There was a relatively small but powerfully built man in the one behind it. At first I never saw the IRF team in that cage. Perhaps they were afraid of him. One evening I spoke to him in Turkish. He talked a lot, but I could only understand a little bit. He was Chechen but came from Dagestan. I tried to imagine what it looked like there. I think he said he was a wrestler. But it must have been some unusual form of wrestling. Using his hands, he explained that you weren't allowed to touch your opponent's legs. I liked the man.

I don't want to reveal too many personal details about him. Today I know that he's back in prison. After being released from Guantanamo and sent home, the Russians arrested him at the airport. They trumped up some accusation against him and threw him in jail. I've been told he was sentenced to fourteen years. He is named after an Arab prophet. It's a common name. I'll call him Isa—the Arab name for the prophet Jesus. In Christianity, Jesus is the messiah. In Islam, he's a major prophet, whose return we are still awaiting. I hope that the Chechen will return some day, too, after he's been freed.

Isa was a funny guy. He was always smiling and making faces, although that was forbidden. He didn't give a damn about the guards or the IRF team. He stood up and exercised when he felt like it. He was unbelievably strong. He could do standing backflips. Once he showed me just how powerful he was.

"Psst," I heard him whisper.

Isa was sitting Indian-style and motioned for me to edge over toward him.

"Psst . . ."

"*Evet*?" I asked in Turkish. Yes?

Isa grinned.

"Ha?"

Isa raised his arms and bent his upper body over sideways toward the cage door. He grabbed a vertical iron bar. I could hardly believe my eyes. Bracing himself on one elbow, his legs walked through the air in slow motion, as if suspended by an invisible rope. Then he straightened both of his arms so that his entire body was suspended off the ground horizontally. I wouldn't have thought that was possible. I'd never witnessed such strength and body control. Isa held this position for a couple of seconds, then carried out the same slow-motion movements in reverse, until he was once again sitting Indian-style on the ground.

I was thrilled.

"Eh?" said Isa, grinning with joy like a child. He slapped his thighs.

I applauded, as though I'd just witnessed a magic trick.

The IRF team came and beat him up terribly. Shortly thereafter they sprayed my cage with pepper spray, the door opened, and it was my turn. I rolled up into a ball as best I could on the ground. At least, I thought, the beating was worth it.

Another time Isa gave me a present. It was after dark and the guards were doing their rounds, so no one was talking.

"Psst," I heard Isa whispering again.

I looked over. He wasn't asleep yet.

"*Hediye*," he whispered. That's Turkish for gift.

In his hand I saw a ball of rolled up paper. I was curious. Was there something to eat inside?

"What's in it?" I asked.

"*Hediye*," he said.

He waited until the guards had passed by his cage. He flicked the paper through the empty cage toward me. It bounced off the fence and landed on the ground, but I succeeded in getting it through the chain link. I opened it and was startled to see to a giant, disgusting, exotic-looking worm. It was neon green, yellow and red, with legs like a millipede and pincers like a scorpion. The worm looked really dangerous. Its colors were like a pretty piece of graffiti art. It quickly crawled from the paper and onto my hand. I let it drop. It writhed on the ground, and I grabbed a flip-flop and tried to crush it. Isa laughed himself sick. He was lying on his back holding his stomach in his hands. Then the IRF team came.

Isa was full of such stunts. When the guards yelled at him, when they threatened and tried to scare him, he would roll up on the ground and laugh. That got the guards really mad. But Isa would just point at them and laugh. As if to say, "Look at how their faces get red when they're yelling."

At Camp X-Ray, there were also female guards—just as there had been in Afghanistan, serving in many capacities except on the IRF teams. There were whites, blacks, and Latinas. The guards were frequently rotated, but I soon came to know most of them. I often saw Cecil Stewart, but he never talked to me. I had the feeling some of the guards would have liked to talk with some of the prisoners. "Sorry," those guards would say. "I can't talk to you. They're watching me." They were under surveillance. It was an iron law that guards weren't to talk to the prisoners. They weren't allowed to treat us like human beings.

I learned the names of two other guards. I will call him Johnson. His specialty was kicking on the cage doors while we prayed. He did this over a course of months. He was known for it.

Once I called him by his name.

"Mr. Johnson, please TP."

That made him mad. Instead of giving me some toilet paper, he sent in the IRF team. The guards patrolled around the clock in twelve-hour shifts. Their boots were always crunching somewhere on the gravel. The only time you didn't hear the sound was at night—because of the loud music. In Charlie, they patrolled the corridors between the cages in pairs, while the others sat somewhere and drank coffee. The sharpshooters watched us from the guard towers.

There were signs in Arabic, English, and Persian on the chain-link fence. "Escape is pointless. Sniper surveillance round the clock." But there was no way we could get out of the cages. The fence was made of thick chain link, with the links welded together. One evening, however, I witnessed a scene that made me think.

It was already dark by the time our guard shoved our paper plates through the opening in the cage doors. Cold gruel and a slice of bread. His mind must have been elsewhere because he also shoved a plate into the empty cage between me and Isa. Maybe he thought its occupant was away being interrogated.

Isa ate his food. Then he turned in my direction. I saw him tear the fence in a certain spot. He bent the wire and loosened, bit by bit, the solder. It sounded like a seam of thread popping. The hole was maybe ten or fifteen inches in diameter so that his arm and half his shoulder fit through the opening. Isa grabbed the plate of gruel from the neighboring cage. He replaced it with his empty plate and sealed up the hole in the chain link so that no one would notice a thing. The chain link fences were full of dents from the batons and prisoners wrestling with the IRF teams.

Isa laughed and ate his second helping of gruel.

Then the guards came to collect the plates. They threw them in a plastic garbage bag. I held out my plate through the opening. In the cage next door, the guard retrieved the empty plate and moved on to Isa, who also handed his plate through. Suddenly the guard stopped. He turned around and looked at the empty cage. He looked at his garbage bag, at Isa, and then at me. He scratched his head.

"I saw who ate that plate of food," I said.

The guard approached my cage.

"Who?"

"You know Lee [not his real name]?"

"Yeah . . ."

"Lee was here. He ate the plate of food and then left it."

"I know Lee is crazy," said the guard. "But he's not that crazy."

"Then you tell me who ate it," I said.

He shrugged. Then he moved on to collect plates form the other prisoners.

Lee was the third guard whose name I knew. He was Asian, and the other guards used to make jokes at his expense. Lee treated us just as badly as his colleagues, and so we often made fun of him, too.

Isa was grinning from ear to ear.

Until that point, I'd never thought about trying to escape. But after I saw how Isa had torn a hole in the chain-link fence—it got me to thinking. If he'd made it bigger, he could have slipped through. There was a possibility to escape. You had to be very strong. But if Isa could do it, couldn't I as well?

Then I would have to climb over the next fence. It was maybe twelve feet high. There was barbed wire on top that you'd have to get through. But what was the story with the perimeter fence?

That night I dreamt of Faruk, a friend of mine from Bremen. I dreamt of how he was consumed by the drugs he took, how he tried to prove how tough he was by beating people up. And I then I dreamt of him looking me in the eye as if to say: Help me! You're my friend!

It was dark when I woke up. I heard the noises of the animals, and I thought about Faruk. I had failed him as a friend. I thought about Bremen. I asked myself how I had come to be sitting in this cage. Actually, I thought, everything started with a joke Selcuk had made about my beard.

Camp X-Ray at Guantanamo Bay, Cuba, during in-processing of detainees to the temporary detention facility on January 14, 2002. Department of Defense photo.

A shower stall adjacent to the recreation and exercise area at Camp Delta, Guantanamo Bay, Cuba on December 3, 2002. Department of Defense photo.

A detention unit at Camp Delta, Guantanamo Bay, Cuba, on December 3, 2002. Department of Defense photo.

Detainees and Military Police at Camp X-Ray at Guantanamo Bay, Cuba, during in-processing to the temporary detention facility on January 11, 2002. They are still wearing the goggles, face masks and soundproof headphones from the flight to Cuba. Department of Defense photo.

Camp X-Ray at Guantanamo Bay, Cuba on January 11, 2002. Department of Defense photo.

An aerial view of Camp Bravo at Guantanamo Bay, Cuba. Department of Defense photo.

U.S. Army Military Police escort a detainee in an orange jumpsuit to his cell in Camp X-Ray at Guantanamo Bay, Cuba, on January 11, 2002. Department of Defense photo.

Camp X-Ray, shown here under construction, Guantanamo Bay, Cuba, January 2002. Department of Defense photo.

Murat Kurnaz, age 16.

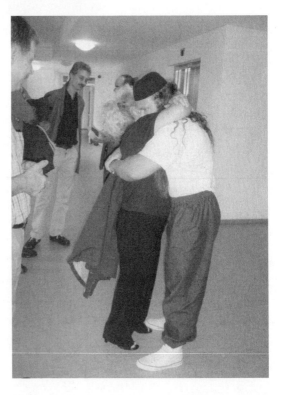

Murat and his mother, Rabiye Kurnaz, after his release from Guantanamo in August, 2006.

VI

BREMEN,
HEMELINGEN

I WAS BORN IN 1982 IN THE MATERNITY WARD OF A HOSPITAL in Bremen. My family rented a top-floor apartment in the working-class district of Hemelingen. When I was twelve, my father bought a row house on a small side street. There were lots of jobs in the area. There was a large meat-packing factory, a soft-drink plant, the Bremen public utilities company, and a company that makes silverware called Wilkens & Sons. The district was a city unto itself, made of red-brick buildings with towers and gables. There were countless derelict warehouses and factory buildings along the Weser River, which separated Hemelingen from the rest of Bremen. My father worked for Mercedes, as did most of the Turkish men in the area.

He did the night shift as a metalworker. It was a hard job. He'd been on the assembly line since the mid-1970s, working the whole night through. The assembly line never stopped—he didn't even have time to scratch his head. For that reason, it was always quiet in my house. We always had to whisper so we wouldn't wake up my father. We only spoke to each other in normal voices after 9 PM, when he would drive off to the factory in his Mercedes.

I also worked for Mercedes during some of my vacations—in the carpenter's workshop and in the cleaning department. Mercedes was a world all its own. The factory halls were so big that everyone used bicycles or golf carts to get around. They had their own carpentry shop, cleaning service, and electricians' division—even their own fire department. Almost all of the employees lived in Hemelingen.

Our district, with its fruit-and-vegetable merchants, kebab shops, and tea salons, began directly behind the Sebaldsbrück train station. From miles away you could tell, by the jungle of satellite dishes on the roofs and next to the apartment windows, that the district was almost entirely Turkish. The sky above the Weser was often cloudy from the fumes of the utilities company.

There was the Sölen kebab stand, the Sultan Travel Agency, the Foreign Workers' Association and the bridge over the train tracks. As a small boy, whenever I would cross the bridge with my father, he would lift me over the railing and hold me on the narrow concrete strip at the edge of the abyss, trying to scare me. "You're going to fall," he'd joke, but he always held me tight in his grasp. There was the Tokcan Market and the bakery where my mother would send me in the afternoon to fetch bread and some baklava. And then the Aladin Discotheque, which was famous for its laser show, one of the biggest discos in Germany. A lot of my friends worked there, including my uncle Ekram who was a bouncer.

I went to school in Glockenstrasse, or "Bell Street," after which the school was named. My friend Orhan lived right around the corner. Back then I also had a Chinese friend whose parents ran the Chinese restaurant at the end of our street. We played together. He'd speak Chinese and I'd speak Turkish, but as kids we didn't need a common language to understand one another. Sometimes his parents would invite me over for dinner and I found it very exotic. I first learned German in kindergarten—almost all of the pupils came from Turkish families. I had a crush on one of the girls. Often I'd convince her to play "family" with me.

She was the mother, and I was the father. But after kindergarten, she went back to Turkey with her parents.

Every afternoon, either with Orhan or on my own, I'd ride my bike to the industrial part of town. I'd pedal under the autobahn overpass, past the vacant fields with the abandoned trailers and into the industrial area. That was my favorite spot to play. You could climb on the cranes and on the heaps of sand and gravel. I used to slide down them on my belly like we used to do in Dédé's hazelnut grove in Kusca. There were old barges on the sides of the Weser, loaded up with sand, gravel, and giant crates. Fishermen stood in the shallow, marshy water. We kids played everywhere, and sometimes they would even let us hop onto the barges. Abandoned trailers were parked alongside uneven paths full of potholes. We cleaned them up and made them look nice again. They were our homes. That's where we played.

I went everywhere by bike. I knew every corner, every abandoned ship, and every three-foot-high roll of cable. There was a junkyard full of metal ship containers and broken furnaces. They were as big as caves. I fooled around between the train tracks. It smelled of either diesel fuel or coffee, depending on whether the wind was blowing in from the wharves or from the coffee factory where they roasted the imported beans.

Below the factory was the spot where I used to go swimming. The ground around the electrical house in front of the wharf was full of rabbit droppings. There, on the slope leading down to the lake, were blackberry bushes surrounded by chain-link fences. I climbed over them, hid in the bushes and ate blackberries. In the evening, the rabbits came out to play. The place got really romantic in the evenings. The factories closed their gates, but the yellow lights stayed on and were reflected in the water. During the day, the machines growled, there was noise everywhere from behind the fences, and thick clouds of steam and smoke rose from the chimneys—but at night, everything was peaceful and quiet. I was alone with the rabbits and the yellow lights.

Sometimes Uncle Ekram came with me to the Weser. He was my mother's younger brother, and I adored him. Uncle Ekram was a funny guy and an adventurer. He taught me how to ride a bike when I was little. Later, we'd go fishing together along the Weser. He'd been in prison once in Cologne. He was very strong. He could pick me up with one hand and hold me over his head, even when I was twelve.

I never found it a disadvantage to be a foreigner. As a kid, it was great to be able to speak two languages. I could have both Turkish and German friends. With my Turkish friends, I could play along the banks of the Weser until it got dark. The German kids had to be home earlier, and many weren't allowed to go to the industrial part of town. They were only allowed to play in their yards or inside their homes. I didn't like that. In the summer, Turkish families spend almost all their time outside.

We were different. We Turkish boys used to play fight. It was completely normal to punch someone. German kids weren't used to it. They immediately took it seriously and started crying or got insulted. Our families and traditions were also very different. We had scores of uncles, aunts, siblings, and cousins. We didn't celebrate Christmas and Easter. We celebrated Eid ul-Adha, the Festival of Sacrifice after the Hajj (pilgrimage to Mecca), and Eid ul-Fitr, the end of the fasting month of Ramadan, when we would gorge ourselves on sweets.

For the Festival of Sacrifice, I would accompany my father to the butcher, and we would select a lamb. We blindfolded the animal. "Bismillah," my father would say. In the name of Allah. Our animals had to be killed by halal slaughtering. As its blood drains out, the animal doesn't feel any pain. The Prophet Mohammed ordered that the knives we use be as sharp as possible. A portion of the meat is supposed to be given to needier people, but most families would just send money to Turkey.

After grade school, I went to the Parseval High School in the Sebaldsbrück district. At the age of eight, I started doing judo. But soon I wanted more. I was fascinated with martial arts, Bruce Lee, and kung fu. Lots of Turkish kids go to karate and kickboxing schools as well as to regular fitness studios. It's an important part of our culture in Germany. All of our uncles and older brothers worked out. Uncle Ekram showed me how to do one-arm push-ups. He told me he'd give me ten Marks if I learned how to do them. I practiced until I could do no more.

A friend of mine even became a European Champion in kickboxing. He was a year older than me, and we were all proud, my friends and I, that he coached us. For a while I joined a boxing club. I was good, but my thoughts were always elsewhere.

After working out, we'd hang out with the girls in the Hemelingen Youth Club. All I thought about back then was which disco had the best-looking girls. With German girls, being a foreigner wasn't a disadvantage. I also had Turkish girlfriends, but problems would quickly arise with them. They weren't allowed to have boyfriends—let alone have sex—before they were married. For me, however, what was written in the Koran was one thing, and what I thought was right was another.

Boxing ceased to interest me by the time I was sixteen. Then I discovered bodybuilding. I already had barbells at home. I'd work out before breakfast, and in the afternoon I'd go to the gym. At the age of seventeen, I could press over three hundred pounds—almost twice my own weight.

If someone had encouraged me back then, I could have gone places with my weightlifting. But I wasn't interested. I wanted to build up my triceps and shoulders. I wanted to look good, have big muscles, and be strong. I had a five o'clock shadow and had put on a lot of bulk. I was very strong for someone my age. Once, at the age of fourteen, I had to appear in court because I had beaten up someone who was over thirty. Things happen.

One day we went go-cart racing. Most of my buddies were already sixteen or seventeen. Some of us were racing while the others watched. We got a bit wild on the track and rammed each other a couple of times. We just wanted to have fun. We hadn't broken anything or done any damage. Beside the track, there was a glass wall and a ticket counter. After our turn was over, the other members of our group wanted to drive and tried to buy tickets. The woman behind the counter said she wouldn't sell them any tickets because the boss said we hadn't behaved. We promised to be good. The lady smiled and gave us the tickets.

But there was another man at the counter. He was well over six feet tall. He took off his glasses, rolled up his sleeves, and attacked my friends. He was very strong. He took two of them simultaneously and smashed their heads against the glass wall. They defended themselves, but they didn't stand a chance. The rest of us joined in and tried to wrestle the man to the ground. Even my friend, the European Champion, got in on the action. But the man managed to get everyone in a headlock or throw them to one side. So I took a barstool and hit him in the back. He turned around and the second time I caught him in the face. In court, they said I broke his chin.

News of that fight soon got around Hemelingen. Two years later, when I joined the fitness studio, the adult members still remembered it. Soon thereafter, I had a number of jobs. I worked in Bremen and the surrounding area as a bodyguard and a bouncer at concerts, parties, and dance clubs. I was earning good money for a sixteen-year-old. But it was risky. My job was to prevent fights. You have to be able to keep strong people apart and, if necessary, hustle them outside. Since I also worked as a bouncer in a Turkish disco, I had to be prepared for people pulling knives and other weapons. I began to ask myself whether I wanted to risk my life for a couple hundred Marks. But everything went well and I never had any problems.

I wore designer clothes. Jackets by Hugo Boss and designer shoes you could buy cheaply in our district. We were always buying and selling something. Jackets, PlayStations, cell phones; we always wanted to have the latest models. I could afford this because I earned a lot of money for my age. I tried to look good. Uncle Ekram was proud of me.

It was around this time that I met Selcuk. We met through Apollo, my Rottweiler. Selcuk lived on our street with his German girlfriend. I was taking the dog for a walk one evening when Selcuk called down to me from his balcony. He wanted to know what to look out for when you get a dog. I had read a lot about being a good dog owner. Then he asked me where I worked out. Selcuk was eight years older than me, and I felt proud when he suggested we go to the gym together. When I met him several days later, he was carrying a puppy under his arm, a Kangal dog.

We were like two peas in a pod. We lived on the same street, we did the same sport, we took our dogs for walks together along the Weser, and we went to the same disco. Selcuk was as religious as I was in those days, which is to say not very religious. Eventually, we found our way to the Muslim faith at roughly the same time. I was eighteen and had begun my apprenticeship as a shipbuilder.

It was fall 2000, around Ramadan. I hadn't seen Selcuk for two weeks. I fasted during the daytime like all the other Muslims and hadn't shaved for a while. Selcuk rang my doorbell. When he saw me, he laughed.

"What happened to you?" he asked. "Are you going on the *hajj* to Mecca?"

He had a good laugh at my expense. I didn't know what he was talking about.

"You look like a pilgrim."

We both laughed at that, and he left.

But Selcuk's remarks had made me think. Wasn't it part of Islam and our heritage that men grew their beards? Surely, fasting wasn't all that connected us as Muslims. The Prophet Mohammed wore a beard. Was that really funny? I didn't shave for the rest of Ramadan.

More and more Turks started asking me why I was growing a beard. They said I should shave it off. I told them I was a Muslim, and that growing a beard was part of our faith. I didn't really know much more than that. But once I had taken that first step toward Islam, I grew curious. What was our faith exactly? What was it about?

I bought some books about Islam, but I didn't really understand them. I went to our mosque in Hemelingen, the Kuba Mosque. I'd gone there sometimes with my father on Fridays, but I didn't understand the Arabic prayers and rituals.

That was how I began to get interested in religion. The trigger was Selcuk's joke about my beard. But at the same time, I had already begun to notice how my friends in Hemelingen were changing. Faruk and Ilias, for example.

I had known Faruk since childhood. We had played together a lot along the Weser, sometimes getting into fights. His parents were divorced. After the divorce, his mother got together with a new man who didn't want Faruk around, and they sent him to live with his grandmother in Turkey. Two years later, he returned. He'd become a tough guy, someone who tried to solve every problem with violence. His mother threw him out of her apartment. He was sent first to a home and then to reform school. By the time we were both sixteen, he was in love with money. He stole things and often got caught. I felt sorry for him. I ran into him all the time in discos, but no one liked him any more. He had become a criminal and started taking drugs. Sometimes when I looked at him, I felt he was drowning in drugs—that's how absent he seemed.

Ilias, too, was hooked. He had grown up with his mother in Turkey, while his father worked in Germany and was married to a German woman. At the age of twelve, he came to Bremen to live with his father, this woman, and their two children. But he didn't get along with his father. When he got into fights with his German half-siblings, his father always took their side. Ilias was also sent to a home. Those homes couldn't have been very good. A lot of people I knew who went there came out broken. When Ilias got out, he told me he knew people now who made a lot of easy money with drugs. I told him that that wouldn't get him anywhere. And I was right. He was thrown in jail, and when I saw him next, hanging around the train station, he was totally stoned. The police nabbed him and deported him to Turkey. I lost several friends this way. They became criminals and addicted to drugs, and then they were deported.

It wasn't because we were foreigners. Allah creates all human beings so that they need love, regardless of whether they're tough or soft. If a person doesn't get any love, I thought, he becomes hateful and violent as he no longer has any feelings for other people. If you take a puppy away from its mother too soon, it will become a problem dog. Of course, there were cases of foreigners being treated badly in school or by the police, and that could easily get to be too much. Back in Bremen, I started to feel like a foreigner for the first time in my life. Once, when I had to go to a government office for foreign residents to take care of some simple formality, they made me wait outside in the cold for half a day, then they simply sent me home without an explanation. "Come back tomorrow," they said, showing no respect at all. If I had been German, they wouldn't have treated me that way.

Things were easier for me at first because I wasn't as noticeably Turkish as other kids. As a child, I had blond hair and very light skin. And I had a good mother and father. Faruk and Ilias didn't have families any more. But didn't Allah create us to have families and love?

Eventually, I gave up the life I had been leading. The people I knew, even if they had been friends, had started ripping each other off. All anyone was interested in anymore was money so that they could buy the latest stuff—cell phones, GameBoys, and laptops—and they didn't care where they got that money. As a bodyguard, it would have been no problem for me to start selling drugs. I had offers. But I couldn't. Someone would be taking the drugs, and that person would have a mother and a father who would worry about him. Islam, as far as I knew, forbids everything bad in our lives: drugs and alcohol, lying, stealing, and unfaithfulness.

In the winter of 2000, I went to the Kuba Mosque a lot. On holidays, I went to the Abu Bakr Mosque near the main train station on my way home from trade school. It is named after the Prophet's father-in-law. Some Arab and black Muslims also prayed there. One day, a group of Muslims from Jama'at al-Tablighi appeared. They said they represented one of Islam's largest groups. There were five of them, two Turks and three German Muslims. After prayers, I started talking to them. German Muslims? I was both fascinated and ashamed. The German Muslims knew a lot more about Islam than I did. I didn't even know the five prayers that we were supposed to say every day.

From then on, for several months, I saw the *tablighis* almost every day in the mosque. One of them had visited the Mansura Center in Lahore. He talked about it a lot, and I asked him about the school. The *tablighis*, they explained, came from Pakistan. If you wanted to do the Hajj, they said, you had to go to Mecca; if you wanted to learn about Islam, you had to go to Lahore. I read about the *tablighis* on the Internet. One day, they said: Come with us!

They wanted to show me what they did. They approached addicts and homeless people in the train station and other parts of the city and offered them help. We visited people who used to be criminals or addicts and who now, thanks to the *tablighis*, had jobs and families. It wasn't just Turks—there were Germans, too. The *tablighis* got people off the streets and helped them find work. I liked the way they practiced Islam.

I decided that I was going to visit the center in Lahore before I got married that summer. I could have chosen an Islamic school in Turkey or Saudi Arabia. But neither Turkey nor Saudi Arabia interested me. I had only heard good things about the Mansura Center, and I wouldn't need much money in Pakistan. I would learn the language, I thought, somehow.

In the meantime, Selcuk had moved to the Sebaldsbrück district. He'd broken up with his German girlfriend and married a Turkish girl. He also wore a beard now. We met up sometimes on the weekends and prayed in the Kuba Mosque. Once again, we seemed to fit together. Selcuk also wanted to know more about Islam. He had gotten to know the *tablighis* and was going to the mosque even more often than me. I excitedly told him about the school in Pakistan. He listened, saying nothing.

In the summer of 2001, before I went to Turkey, I had told him about my plans to get married, saying that I had probably found a wife. When I got back, I declared I was definitely going to Pakistan.

"If I can work it out, I'll come with you," he said.

Apparently, he wasn't in as much of a hurry as I was.

"If you want to come with me," I said, "then let's go. I want to see this through now. I'm planning to bring my wife to Hemelingen in December. I have to be back by then."

Selcuk hesitated.

"Now or never," I said. "Otherwise I'm going alone."

"You're right," said Selcuk.

We agreed not to tell anyone about what we were planning. The one person we let in on our plans was Ali. I'd met Ali in the Abu Bakr Mosque. He was 35 back then and he also knew Selcuk. He was in the mosque every time we were there. I'd already told him before the summer that I was looking for a *multesima* to marry. Ali had told me everything I needed to know about the ceremony. When I returned from Turkey, he was very happy that I had married Fatima. So I told him about the *tablighis* and our travel plans. At first Ali said nothing. But a couple days later, he took me aside.

"If I can give you some advice, don't go."

He repeated that a number of times.

"I'm not trying to tell you two what to do, but I'd advise against it."

I told him that I liked traveling and didn't see any danger, and he shrugged.

"I hope you know what you're doing."

On September 11, I was at shipbuilding school when the attacks on the World Trade Center in New York and the Pentagon in Washington took place. On my way home, I met a friend who said that a plane had crashed in the United States. That's not so unusual, I said. Why are you telling me this? When I got home, my mother called me into the living room. Come quick, she said. There's something earth-shattering in the United States.

Then I saw the two towers collapsing. As I watched the images being repeated, I knew that this was not an accident. I felt sorry for the people who had been in the buildings. My mother had woken my father up, even though it was still afternoon. I sat in front of the TV for a long time, as if under a spell.

A few days later it was reported that the attack had been carried out by a group led by a terrorist named Osama bin Laden, who was hiding in the mountains of Afghanistan. I didn't think there would be a war with Afghanistan, and my father agreed. They only wanted to capture Osama bin Laden and his cronies. I heard about U.S. preparations for war on the news. But I thought that they would only go into the mountainous region where the terrorists were hiding. Or that the Afghans would give him up. It would work itself out somehow.

I couldn't imagine there was going to be a war. And if that happened, it would be a war between Afghanistan and the United States. I would be in Pakistan. What did Pakistan have to do with Afghanistan? It was a different country. I didn't see why I should change my plans.

For Friday prayers, I went to a Turkish mosque. The imam spoke about the attacks. He said that it should never be allowed to happen again. Selcuk and I called the Pakistani consulate in Berlin and asked about the entry requirements. We got an appointment to apply for visas and we drove to Berlin. The consulate took our passports and mailed them back to us two weeks later with our visas.

I didn't tell my parents about our plans. They would have gotten upset and tried to keep me from going. We're not allowed to contradict our parents—it's part of our faith that we should show them respect; it's laid out explicitly in the Koran. I couldn't tell my mother, she wouldn't have let me go. So I decided to call her from the airport.

I withdrew money from the bank and Selcuk and I went to buy our plane tickets. The only travel agency we knew was located in a shopping center my parents also went to. My mother sometimes ran into her friends there. Some of our relatives also went to the mall to drink coffee and go shopping. If anyone had seen me coming in or out of the travel agency, they would have asked questions. I gave Selcuk 1,100 Marks for my ticket and waited in a Turkish tea salon several streets away.

I called Ali, and he tried to talk us out of our trip. But I already had my return ticket in my pocket and wasn't willing to change my plans. Several days before I left, I sold my cell phone. It was a Nokia phone with a pre-paid German card that wouldn't have worked anyway in Pakistan. We always sold our old cell phones, sometimes once every one or two months, so that we could always have the latest model. What's more, I needed the money. After I returned, I thought, I'd get a new cell phone.

Selcuk and I agreed to leave at night. The closer our day of departure came, the more excited I got. I had a bad conscience because of my parents. I would have liked to say good-bye to them, but that was impossible.

Then it occurred to me how I could at least give my mother a hug. I knew my parents and my brother Ali were visiting a family in Sebaldsbrück, but they were sure to come home before midnight.

"Ana, my back aches."

"It's late. I'll give you a massage in the morning."

"Salam alaikum," I said.

"Alaikum salam," she said.

We checked our bags at the ticket counter, received our boarding passes, and went to the passport control with our visas. The customs officer scanned my passport and motioned for me to go through. But he didn't let Selcuk pass. After he'd entered Selcuk's details into his computer, he said:

"You're not allowed to leave the country. There's a fine you haven't paid."

"What kind of fine?"

"For bodily injury," said the customs officer. "If you want to leave Germany, you have to pay the fine."

I was already in the waiting area. I heard Selcuk try to clear up the matter with the customs officer. Selcuk said he wanted to call a lawyer.

"That's fine," said the customs officer. "Come this way."

Another officer asked me if I wanted to take the plane or not. The bus to the aircraft was waiting for us—all the other passengers were checked in. Our names were called via loudspeaker. We were to proceed immediately to the boarding gate. There was no way Selcuk would make it.

Everything happened so quickly.

"I'll call my brother," Selcuk said. "He'll pay the fine for me, if there's no other choice."

"Okay."

"I'll take the next plane," Selcuk said. "We'll meet at Karachi airport. Wait for me there."

"Okay," I said. "I'll wait for you."

Selcuk followed the customs officer, and I went to the bus.

I never saw Selcuk again.

VII

GUANTANAMO BAY, CAMP X-RAY

"ALI MIRI?"

"Yes, Ali Miri. Who is Ali Miri?"

"A friend of mine from Bremen . . ."

"What do you know about him?"

"Not much. He's nice. He's married. With kids . . ."

"Where did you meet him?"

"In the mosque . . ."

"Which mosque?"

"At the main train station. I went there on Fridays after shipbuilding school . . ."

"The Abu Bakr Mosque?"

"Yes, that's the one."

"Where does he work?"

"I think he's on welfare."

The German-speaking American seemed impatient. He smoked a lot and played with his camera-pen. I was not allowed to sit down during the interrogation. I was chained by my hands and feet to the ring in the floor so that I could only kneel or stand half bent-over. If I knelt, I could straighten my back, but my knees hurt. If I bent over, the blood would start flowing into my legs again, but I had to look up at the American, and that made my neck hurt. But what could I do, tell him, "I want to go home now"?

The interrogation lasted several hours. I was starving, thirsty, and sweating from every pore, as though I had run for miles. Every fiber of my body hurt. The American asked the same questions over and over. It had been a long time since he'd told any amusing stories. He spat out orders, yelled, and called me a terrorist. He'd asked about my friends and schoolmates, naming names and telephone numbers. One of them was my coach at the fitness studio. Suddenly he had hit upon Ali. I was surprised.

"Ali Miri was your imam," said the American. "The deputy imam of the Abu Bakr Mosque."

"The imam? No, he wasn't an imam. I know that he taught children. I only saw him praying like everyone else in the mosque. The man who led the prayers was someone else."

"He was your secret imam. Your leader."

"He wasn't a leader."

"He encouraged you to become fighters."

"No."

"He made you into a Taliban, admit it!"

"No, he was my friend."

"He called you nine times before your departure. What did he tell you?"

"Nine times? I don't know anything about that."

"Don't lie!"

"It may be that he called me. He wanted to convince me not to go to Pakistan. . . ."

Ali had tried to call me nine times? We had talked on the phone once or twice before I left, but I remembered calling *him*. Had he tried to reach me after I had already left?

"You called Ali Miri from Pakistan!"

"No, I didn't call anyone from Pakistan. No, wait a minute. I did call Selcuk's wife because I wanted to know whether he was still coming. But she hung up on me. Twice."

"What kind of car does Ali Miri drive?"

"What kind of car? A station wagon. A big station wagon."

"Brand?"

I don't know. It was a big station wagon."

"Color?"

"Light-colored. Maybe gray . . ."

"Does he preach against America? Did he try to stir you up?"

"I've never heard him say anything about that. He never talked about these things."

The American stood up and fished some photographs from his brief-case. He showed them to me. They were pictures of Ali Miri. They must have been taken somewhere on the street in Bremen. Where did he get these photos? And how did he know that Ali had tried to call me?

"Is that Ali Miri?"

"Yes, that's him. What did he do?"

"That's none of your business."

The American showed me pictures of Ali before he had grown his beard. It was hard to recognize him. But I told him, "Yes, that's Ali," so as not to disagree. Then he said that my plane ticket had been paid for by terrorists.

"My plane ticket? I paid for it myself. I withdrew money from the bank and paid for it. You know that already."

"No, it was paid for with a cash card. It belonged to the father of a Tunisian, Sofyen Ben Amor. You were friends with him, too."

"I don't know him. Who?"

"Sofyen Ben Amor!"

"I know two *Suf*yans in Bremen. I don't know whether or not one might have been Tunisian. If you show me a photo, maybe I'll recognize him."

"Sofyen Ben Amor had contacts to terrorists in Hamburg!"

"I don't know anything about that . . ."

"Don't lie! He paid for your ticket! In a travel agency called Go Travel!"

"Selcuk paid for my ticket!"

I told the American why I hadn't gone with Selcuk into the travel agency. I couldn't understand how this other man could have possibly paid for my ticket. I went with Selcuk to the shopping center alone and had waited in a nearby tea salon for him. Selcuk didn't have anyone with him when he returned. He didn't give me back my money. Why should he have kept it? There was never any talk of a Tunisian. I didn't know every one of Selcuk's friends and acquaintances, but he hadn't told me he had met anyone in the shopping center, either. And even if he had, why should that guy have paid for my ticket? It didn't make sense. Was the American making everything up? But how then did he know so many details about my life?

I didn't know what I was supposed to think. But I noticed he was trying to set me a trap. Only now—months after they had asked about my cell phone for the first time, my bank account, and Selcuk—did I realize that they had known everything about me from the very beginning. They weren't interested in the fact that I had never been to Afghanistan and was innocent. I didn't stand a chance. I knew that now.

———

What does someone do who's cooped up in a cage all day? I sat. Sometimes cross-legged, sometimes with my legs stretched out. I waited for food. I prayed when the time came. I waited and I sat, legs bent, legs straight. When I thought the guards weren't looking, I got up for a second and stretched my legs. Or tried to speak with the other prisoners. Sometimes I'd do a couple push-ups. I used to be able to do a hundred. Now I had problems just supporting my weight with my arms. More than five were out of the question anyway. The guards would notice and send in the IRF team.

I estimated that I had lost around forty or fifty pounds. Every few week we got new clothes, and though I used to need an XXL, small or medium now fit me. One of the other men was little more than skin and bones. He must have weighed less than ninety pounds. I spied him from a distance and remembered seeing him once in Kandahar. He was much bigger back then. Whenever I looked over, he was sitting. He never got up. Maybe he could no longer stand up. Sometimes, in a cage like that, you entertain stupid thoughts.

I began to pick at the threads of my blanket. Before long I had a sixteen-foot-long thread in my hands. Every now and then, we would get Emaries again. I had saved the package in which the crackers came. I filled it up with dirt and pebbles. I tied it to the thread and threw it several feet away into the corridor between the caves. You could hardly see the thread. I waited until Lee came.

"Lee, can you help me?"

"What?"

"My neighbor threw me some crackers, but they landed in the corridor."

"That's against the rules! It's not allowed! Where are they?"

"Over there. Can you see them?"

Lee wanted to pick up the package and throw them away.

I tugged the thread.

"My God!" said Lee.

He tried to pick up the package again, but I pulled the thread.

"What's going on?"

I pulled the package into my cage. Lee still hadn't noticed the thread. He was really afraid. He ran back to the other guards and kicked up a fuss. All the prisoners who had been watching started to laugh. When the other guards came, I showed them the thread. They laughed, too, and said I would have to be punished. The IRF team came, and they took my blanket and mattress away. Two days later they gave them back.

Why did I do this?

Lee treated us badly. He yelled at us, made fun of us, and pounded against our cage doors while we prayed, just like Johnson. He was simply stupid. But he wasn't as bad as Johnson, who beat Abdul on the hands when he was trying to hoist himself on to his bucket. Johnson was a red-faced, bald man whose eyes twinkled as though he was on drugs. He tried to play the tough guy. He particularly had it in for Isa since the Chechen was always grinning and making fun of the guards. The IRF visited him more often than any of the other prisoners now. And Isa fought back every time. Sometimes, he succeeded in throwing one of the IRF soldiers to the ground or hitting one of them in the visor.

It's strange, but with time, you grow numb even to blows. Blows from the IRF team were the basic form of punishment in Camp X-Ray. At that point there were no solitary-confinement cells—they were still being built. They would also punish us by beating us and then chaining our hands and feet, connecting those chains with a third one. You couldn't move your arms, they were pressed to your body. Then they'd leave you sitting there like that and take away your blanket and the thin mattress. It could take days before they'd unshackle you.

I couldn't see any rhyme or reason in their punishments, though I understood that the IRF team would beat me if I dared to play a joke on Lee. There was no way they could sit back and tolerate something like that. The IRF was called in on numerous occasions when the guards had seen me feeding breadcrumbs to iguanas or birds. I could understand that as well. And, of course, the IRF team came when they caught me doing push-ups.

But most of the time I didn't know why I was being punished. Sometimes they just seemed to invent excuses. For instance, they claimed I had tried to hide my blanket, although I hadn't touched it the entire day. Why would I want to hide my blanket? And where? Under the mattress? Or I was punished for dirtying my shirt, even if it was clean. Sometimes, the thugs came without any excuse at all—in the middle of the night, in the afternoon, or at breakfast time.

I gradually came to realize that punishment itself was the rhyme and reason for their behavior—there was no avoiding it. The point of punishment was to constantly humiliate us. It was the same when we took showers. Every time the soldier who operated the water supply thought up something new. Even if I lathered myself up as quickly as possible, the water would still be cut off before I had washed off the soap. Once I was brought out to take a shower and the soldier turned on the water while my guard was still unlocking the cage. As I was about to dash under the hose, he turned it off. "Your time's up," he said. I hadn't gotten a single drop of water. That really made me mad. I wanted to hit someone.

But that was exactly what they were trying to achieve, and I suppressed my anger. Sometimes weeks would go by without them letting us take a shower. We didn't have the right to one.

———————————

Then I got a new neighbor in Charlie-Charlie 4. It was a nice surprise. The escort team dragged him into the empty cage, which since my arrival had only been occupied by a dead cockroach that decomposed a little more every day. It was Salah from Oman, whom I'd met in my jail cell in Pakistan. Kemal, who had also shared that cell with us, was put in Charlie as well, but he was in Charlie-Alpha. I could only communicate with him via hand gestures. They both arrived on the same day. Salah stretched his finger through the chain link, and I shook it.

I was happy to see Salah because he was like an older brother to me. He was a quiet guy with five children. I knew from our previous encounter that he had gone to university in the United States, but I didn't know what he had studied, and Salah didn't like talking about his family and his life before Guantanamo. In prison it's better not to open up too much about yourself. But I was able to learn English from him.

At some point they hung a crest of arms on the fence. It was impossible to overlook. It featured a five-cornered building, with a black star inside it with an ocean and a horizon behind it. In the middle, you saw the outline of Guantanamo. On top of it all stood the words: Honor Bound to Defend Freedom.

I asked Salah what that meant.

Salah translated things for me, also from Arabic, so that I could understand what the others said. Thanks to him I was able to get new information for the first time in a long time.

Someone had talked to the Red Cross. According to them, the Americans said we would have to stay in the camp permanently. Salah knew the specifics. He said that Donald Rumsfeld believed we could be kept in these cages indefinitely and without a trial. That was the news. But Allah would decide whether he wanted to send us home or not. Allah was on the side of the good people and not of Donald Rumsfeld. I mustn't worry.

I learned my first Arabic suras. An imam was now leading our prayers. He was a dark-skinned fifteen-year-old who had learned the Koran by heart. His cage was far from mine, but it was still in Charlie. I saw him sometimes when I was taken to the showering cage. He had a clear, loud voice. His prayers varied in length depending on which of the suras he recited.

A few of the prisoners had English versions of the Koran in their cages. They hung them on thin threads from the chain-link fencing since the Koran must never get dirty or lie on the ground. Arabic editions weren't permitted. "Maximum security!" we joked. There could have been something dangerous in it. I wanted a Koran, too, but the guards refused to bring me one. One of them said they had run out. Another pointed to a prisoner who did have one and said, Ask him! A third guard said, What am I, a Muslim? I don't have one. When the young dark-skinned imam called us to prayer, I tried to repeat the words in my heard or whisper them softly.

———

One time there was a long, tortured cry. I turned around. There was a second and then a third cry, but they sounded different from the cries of people being beaten. It was the long and frightening wail of death. Through the chain-link fencing I could see a guard in the cage of one of the Arab prisoners. I immediately knew what had happened.

We were searched every day. They even searched the Korans. The guards grabbed the books by their spines and shook them to see if anything was concealed in the pages. This guard must have thrown the Koran on the ground—otherwise the prisoner wouldn't have howled like that. I saw the guard trampling on something.

Some of the prisoners sprang to their feet. A terrible wailing arose. One by one, all the prisoners were losing their cool. "Allahu akbar!" they yelled. "Don't do that!" I screamed. The guard continued trampling on the Koran. It was as though lightning had struck in a zoo. Some of the prisoners tried to kick down the cage doors, others shook the fencing, trying to tear or bite their way through the chain links. Suddenly, the guard was afraid. He left the Koran on the ground and ran away. The other guards also beat a hasty retreat from Charlie Block. They ran through the corridors and hid behind the second chain-link fence.

The prisoners were getting wilder. They screamed and wailed and kicked against the fencing and spun around in circles like dervishes. Some of them were rolling around on the ground. The clamor spread like wildfire to the other blocks. I heard yelling and crying from Alpha and Foxtrot. A short time later, Humvees, jeeps, and trucks arrived. Soldiers marched forward slowly encircling the camp. They wore bullet-proof vests and carried machine guns. Kneeling or lying on their stomachs, they trained high-caliber rifles on us.

They took aim. I looked up at the watchtowers. The sharpshooters also had us in their sights. The situation was alarming. A massacre could have happened at any minute. The only thing that had to happen, I thought, was for someone to break out of his cage.

What was Isa doing? He wasn't tearing at his cage door. He was just standing there with a clenched fist, smiling.

They turned on the floodlights. I heard one of the prisoners call out something in Arabic. I didn't understand what he said, but the howling began to ebb. Most of the prisoners calmed down and let go of their cage doors. Some of them were already beginning to sit back down. I sat down too, thinking it was the best thing to do in the situation. The Arab prisoner whose Koran had been defiled picked the Holy Book up off the ground. Again, someone called out something that I didn't understand. A number of long minutes passed. The soldiers still had us in their sights.

Then the IRF teams came. They sprayed pepper spray in all the blocks. I shut my eyes and pressed my hands to my face. I heard them running on the gravel. "Hurry, hurry." I heard cage doors being opened. "Get up! Hurry!" The sounds of chains, blows, screams. I spread my fingers and could see Kemal emptying his water bucket on soldiers who were beating up a prisoner in the adjacent cage. The soldiers stormed into Kemal's cage. When he was on the ground, his neighbor poured the content of his toilet bucket on the soldiers.

Then I saw other prisoners emptying their toilet buckets on the IRF teams. The team in Kemal's cage left him on the ground and began beating up his neighbor. When they were through with him, they returned to Kemal, grabbed his feet, and dragged him off. A lot of the prisoners were taken away. Then the soldiers returned and beat up the rest.

The IRF teams had a busy night. It was morning before they stopped. They looked pretty worn out. I was lucky. This time around they didn't visit me. Maybe they were just tired.

The following day some of the prisoners refused to take their breakfast. Others accepted the paper plates but didn't eat anything. When the guards came to my cell, I shook my head. Salah wouldn't eat anything either, and even Abdul didn't touch his plate. We weren't acting on a plan. It just happened spontaneously. By noon, no one in Charlie was eating anything. That afternoon we heard from Bravo that all of the blocks were on hunger strike. In the morning, at noon, and in the evening, the guards came with paper plates and Emaries, but we all refused to take them.

Kemal never returned.

On the fourth day of our hunger strike, the general who was in charge of Guantanamo in the early days arrived and talked with one of the English-speaking prisoners. The prisoner refused to stand up in the general's presence. The general took his cap off and sat on the ground in the corridor in front of the cage. At that moment, I realized that we were not utterly powerless. We could bring them to their knees if we all went on hunger strike! They didn't want us to die. But I didn't understand why the general had taken off his cap. Was he trying to signal that he wasn't on the job, that he wanted to speak to the prisoner as a human being?

The general and the prisoner talked.

The general was surrounded by a dozen or so high-ranking officers. They had stopped in their tracks. They didn't seem to like it that the general was sitting on the ground. The general asked why we had stopped eating. The prisoner explained how important the Koran was to us and what it meant. The general said he would punish the soldier who had defiled the Koran. When he got up and started to leave Charlie with the officers, he passed by my cage. He slowed down and looked me over. Probably because of my fair skin, I thought. I spoke to him.

"What happen?" I asked.

The general's answer was long, and I didn't understand very much. After he left, Salah explained:

"He said he'll ensure personally that something like that doesn't happen again."

We talked at length amongst ourselves in the blocks that day, and the guards let us. Some of the prisoners said they didn't believe the Americans. They suggested returning their copies of the Koran because they'd rather not have the book at all than risk it being defiled again. Others thought we should wait and see. In the end, we all agreed that we had to get organized and elect a leader. That evening, the first group of prisoners resumed eating. I decided not to, although I was very hungry. A guard came to me and asked why I still didn't want to eat.

"Look over there," he said, pointing to a man with a cup in his hand. "You'll even get some warm tea if you start eating again."

He had to be joking, I thought. After he left, I found out that they had in fact distributed tea. What an idiot! Did he really think he could bribe us with a cup of tea? I couldn't understand who the American guards thought they were.

A few days later, the general reappeared, he wanted to negotiate. He asked for our conditions. The prisoner who spoke English demanded that the guards no longer be allowed to handle and search through our Korans. We didn't want our private parts searched. And we didn't want to be frisked by female guards. If he agreed to all that, we would start eating again. The general agreed.

That evening I ate some cold rice and crackers. They tasted great.

After the incident with the Koran, we went ahead and elected a leader. All of the prisoners were allowed to nominate a candidate. It was a secret vote—the Americans knew nothing about it. It took several weeks because the vote was strictly oral, the preliminary results passed from cage to cage. Out of five hundred prisoners, ten men were chosen, and suggestions were collected and evaluated. Those ten men chose three other men, who in turn elected our leader. We called him the emir. No one but the three men who had elected him knew who he was. Officially this man was not our leader. He chose a spokesperson to deal with the Americans and to appear as our leader. In that way, the real emir could remain in the background, undetected.

We strung the Americans along. We acted as though we had elected an emir, the spokesperson, and let his name be known. Before long the spokesperson disappeared for months. The Americans thought they had broken our resistance, and there wouldn't be any more hunger strikes. But the real emir was still making the decisions behind the scenes. He collected opinions from all the prisoners' representatives and decided what the figurehead emir would tell the Americans.

We wanted to put an end to the defilements of the Koran. We wanted the Americans to respect our faith and stop playing the U.S. national anthem during our prayers. We wanted to restrict the level of torture and get medicine for some of the wounded prisoners. Sometimes the

Americans seemed to accede to our demands, for example regarding medicine, but of course we had no way of knowing what exactly it was they were giving the sick prisoners. We wanted them to treat the sick, elderly, and handicapped prisoners more respectfully. We wanted proper food.

Later, each block chose its own emir. Eventually I also became a block emir because I came to speak not only good English but other languages used by the prisoners. In Bremen, I had studied English in school, but the language didn't interest me because I didn't have any use for it. In Kandahar and Guantanamo, I wanted to learn English so that I could understand the Americans and defend myself during interrogations. I wanted to learn Arabic so that I could read the Koran and understand the other prisoners. I learned English from my interrogators and from Salah, Uzbek from Uzbeks, Farsi from the Afghans, Arabic from Salah and the Saudis, and Italian from the Algerian who had lived in Italy. I wasn't fluent in these languages by any means, but I could make myself understood. And that was very useful in Guantanamo.

When it was my turn to be the emir, I was the contact person for the Americans. I mostly served as emir when I wasn't being transferred or spending time in solitary confinement. They transferred us frequently to prevent us from getting organized, but the more often they moved us, the more quickly information spread among the prisoners.

As an emir I was responsible for whether or not prisoners in my block would go on hunger strike. There were some longer hunger strikes and a lot of shorter ones. I had read that if a man doesn't eat for two weeks, or doesn't drink anything for four or five days, he can die. I believe the doctors in Guantanamo didn't know exactly when a man might die. That's why they were careful during the first hunger strikes—until they found out precisely how long we could last without food or water. One of the prisoners refused to eat for more than a hundred days. At some point he was force-fed. There were always small groups of prisoners or individuals on hunger strikes. Soon the Americans understood our tactics. They didn't seem to care any more if someone hadn't eaten for a couple of weeks. They only came after twenty days or more.

I listened to the prisoners' demands and passed them on to the Americans. Negotiations began. They would make us offers to end the hunger strikes. The negotiations were tough. For example, the Americans offered to remove the Korans from our cages—that was one of our demands. But we would also have to give up our T-shirts. Their offers always included punishments. We were given a choice to either keep our overalls or get medicine for someone who was sick. Either keep our soap and flip-flops or be allowed more showers. The Americans called this making "suggestions." If there wasn't a majority among the prisoners, then I had to decide.

I soon realized that we didn't have any real power. It was just an illusion. It was up to the general alone whether or not there would be negotiations. He was the first and last camp commandant with whom we could at least negotiate religious issues. He kept his word. But this general was replaced, and everything changed overnight.

Still, our leadership system worked. The men who were our official emirs were always being put in solitary confinement. The man that we had first elected in Camp X-Ray remained the real emir without the Americans ever catching on. Indeed, very few of the prisoners knew who the real emir was.

I know his name, but I'm not saying anything. As of 2007 he's still in Guantanamo, and he's still the prisoners' true leader.

VIII

GUANTANAMO BAY, CAMP DELTA

CAMP X-RAY WAS CLOSED IN LATE APRIL 2002.

I was there for three months. During this time, the Americans built Camps 1 and 2 and the isolation ward "India." In April 2002, Camp 1 was opened, and we were transferred there. While we were in Camp 1, they built Camps 3 and 4 and the isolation wards "Romeo," "Quebec," and "Tango." We were then moved to Camp 3, during which time they built Camp 5 and, in 2006, Camp 6. Sometimes we could see the construction sites but we could always hear them since construction work went on around the clock. They had approximately twenty new diesel generators that, when they were on, which was most of the time, made so much noise that we could never sleep for more than a few moments.

The entire facility was called Camp Delta.

———————

One day, buses—they looked like American school buses—stopped in front of the chain-link fences. Soldiers inspected our mouths and ears, bound us and put goggles, soundproof headphones, and gas masks on our heads. We were led to the buses and chained to the floor. There were no seats, and they beat us. After two or three hours, we drove off. It wasn't a long ride. When we arrived in Camp Delta, they removed our goggles.

What a surprise.

The blocks looked as through they were made of metal walls welded together to form a giant container. Inside the containers were the cages, but this time their sides were made of metal grille instead of chain-link fence. The prisoners could see through the lattice, and the guards could keep us under observation at all times. The grille was razor sharp.

I was put in Camp 1, Block Alpha, Cell Alpha-2. At first glance, the cage looked more modern than the one I had occupied in Camp X-Ray. The mattress was no longer on the ground but rested on a bunk bed welded to the wall. Although the cage was no smaller than the one in Camp X-Ray, the bunk reduced the amount of free space to around three-and-a-half feet by three-and-a-half feet. At the far end of the cage, an aluminum toilet and a sink took up even more room. How was I going to stand this?

This was no dog pound. It was a maximum-security cage. Even Isa wouldn't have been able to break anything in it—the cell could have withstood a charging elephant. There were forty-eight of these cages, in two rows of twenty-four, in every block. They were closely surrounded by the walls of the container. The only windows were along the short walls at both ends of the container so that the first and last cells were the only ones to get any real direct sunlight. In Alpha-2, I hardly saw the sun at all.

They had perfected their prison.

At some point during my time in X-Ray, I had stopped noticing the chain-link fence. I could see the sky, the hills and the cacti. Now I saw nothing but metal lattice and the roof. It felt like being sealed alive in a ship container. The only fresh air came though the windows. It was unbearably sticky and hot.

Compared to the provisional facilities in X-Ray, the toilet and the sink looked like the ones in a proper prison. I knew about jails from American movies and Uncle Ekram's anecdotes. I was going to have a tough time, but I told myself I would survive. In a proper prison, there are rules that the guards have follow, an everyday routine, and a prison yard.

I noticed immediately that the new cage was smaller than the old one, and it was clear they couldn't possibly keep us locked up in there twenty-four hours a day. I was convinced that we would sleep there, and then during the day we'd be let out into the yard. It took a few days for me to realize that there was no prison yard. I'd been kidding myself again.

***

After I was released I read in a newspaper that, according to official sources, the cells in Camp Delta measure six-and-a-half by eight feet. That's not accurate. I measured my cage with my hand and arrived at six-and-a-half by seven feet. The difference may not seem that significant, but it is an example of the constant deception. Nothing in the camp is what it seems, nothing is the way the U.S. Army says it is and as it has been reported, filmed, and photographed by journalists. There are cages and interrogation rooms specially constructed for the media. In media reports, you often see things on the bunks that I never once had in Guantanamo: a backgammon board, for example, or books or a bar of chocolate. In all the photos taken of the inside of Camp Delta, there's a Koran hanging on the wall, covered in white cloth and bound by a ribbon. Sometimes we had Korans in the cages, but that was an exception, not the rule, and there certainly weren't any white cloths with ribbons. The fake cells were their attempt to convince people that they respected our faith.

My neighbor was light-skinned like me and spoke very good English. He was a Muslim from a country that borders Germany—I don't want to say which one. He has since been freed, and he has never spoken to the media. He wants to be left alone, and I want his wishes to be respected. I'm going to call him Mani. His native tongue was French, and he could also speak a few words of German.

Mani was maybe two or three years older than me. He was very helpful and taught me the Koran. Both of us now had a Koran, a bilingual edition in Arabic and English. I had asked for one repeatedly, and one day, to my surprise, a guard brought me one. We sat on the floor of our cells, and through the metal lattice Mani taught me how to read the Koran without making mistakes. It was a lot of fun. But whenever Johnson was in the block, he'd kick the door and tell us we weren't allowed to talk.

Mani and I were neighbors for three months. One day he was taken away, and when he returned from what I figured was an interrogation, I asked, "Well, how was it?"

"Great," he said. "I went for a walk." To my astonishment, he told me there was a prison yard in Camp Delta.

"Don't talk nonsense," I said.

But Mani wasn't talking nonsense. Twice a week, the guards had told him, prisoners were allowed out into the yard for fifteen minutes, as long as they weren't serving out a punishment.

A couple of days later, I saw the yard. It was a caged-in area behind the container block. The Americans called it the "rec area," and I estimated it to be twenty-two by thirty-eight feet. I was allowed to pace back and forth there, alone. Prisoners weren't allowed to touch the chain-link fence, and the ground was made of concrete. I couldn't believe my eyes and looked at the guard. Someone told me I had fifteen minutes.

But what did that mean: fifteen minutes? I didn't have a watch, and after a couple of minutes, as was always the case in the showers, my time was up. And what did twice a week mean? I was only let out into the yard once or twice a month at most. The rest of the time they said there was a danger of lightning or hurricanes. But usually the sun was shining—that much I could see through the windows.

One day I took a small, pointed stone from the yard back into my cage. I used it, as surreptitiously and as far away from the door and the guards as I could, to draw a Nine Men's Morris board on my bunk. I made the pieces from toilet paper, tiny balls and tubes. We played the game, and when the guards came we started talking about the Koran. Mani didn't know Nine Men's Morris, so I won the first few games in a row. Then Mani got better.

Though I could now play games and talk about the Koran with Mani, interrogations into the wee hours of the night and the beatings continued. The interrogation rooms in Camp Delta all had mirrors behind which other interrogators sat and cameras recorded the questioning. They kept trying to trick me. Once, one of the interrogators said:

"You know that there were people who were Taliban and are now at home?"

That was true. Word had gotten around that some of the Taliban fighters had already been freed.

"Do you know why?" asked the interrogator. "They're soldiers who fought for their country. We know who they are, and we let them go. But the problem with you is that we don't know who you are. We don't know whether you're Taliban or Al Qaeda. That makes you dangerous. Tell us that you're part of Al Qaeda, and we'll let you go."

Of course it was a trick. Maybe it would have helped if I had confessed to being a Taliban, even if they knew that wasn't true. Then they could have said I was guilty and maybe let me go. But I wasn't giving in to that.

The permanent exhaustion weighed me down like lead in my shoes. It was an iron rule in Camp Delta that all cages were to be searched at least once a day and once at night. They'd kick the door and yell. Stand up and prepare to be shackled.

Although there was nothing to search but the mattress, the ceiling and our flip-flops, they always took their time, shining their flashlights in every corner. They would whistle cheerfully all the while, waking up the other prisoners, and kicking the cage walls and the sink to see if everything was still solid. Searches often lasted a half an hour.

When the guards visited the cages, the fans on the corridor ceiling would be turned on so they wouldn't break a sweat. The fans were as loud as airplane generators. The guards brought chairs along so they could sit down and rest. They talked demonstratively loudly, played cards, and sang songs. When I wasn't being interrogated, I tried to get some sleep, but you can't get any real rest by catnapping. Occasionally they'd return after an hour, wake me up again, and search my cell a second time.

The welded metal plates in the corridor floor were warped from the heat. The guards loved to stomp on the spots where the floor had arched because it made a loud noise. When they lead a prisoner through the corridor, you could hear them from a long way off, and when they came to pick someone up, they'd drop the chains loudly to the floor. With forty-eight prisoners per block, there was always someone coming or going. The fans and diesel generators hummed, and the guards took their keys and scraped them along the metal lattice. In the beginning, I hoped things would change. But after a few months, I knew it would always be like this.

I thought about the birds I had kept as a boy. Sometimes, I felt sorry for them in their cages. In Camp X-Ray, there were always birds. I had fed them with breadcrumbs I concealed from the guards under my clothing and my mattress. At first the birds were shy, but gradually they came to trust me. Some of them—especially the zunzúns, a kind of blue, white, and red hummingbird hardly bigger than a locust—could fly through the chain link fence. Some were even small enough to get into our pens in Camp Delta. I was overjoyed when the first zunzún flew through the lattice of my cage, followed by other zunzúns. I used to talk to the birds about how strange the world was. They used to be in a cage, and I would visit them, and now the situation was reversed.

For the first few months at Camp Delta I wasn't allowed to shower because I was being punished for something. Finally, I was taken to the shower cells. The water came on; I got under it and started to lather up. The soldier turned the water off.

I had had enough.

"Why didn't you give me my two minutes?" I yelled at the guards.

"Your time is up," he said. "Get dressed."

"You didn't give me two minutes!" I insisted.

"I decide how long you get to shower."

"You have to give me two minutes. If there are rules, why don't you follow them?"

"You don't have any say here."

"Rules are rules, and you have to follow them!"

"Back in your cage. Get going!"

I took the small piece of soap to the lattice and squeezed my hand so that it popped out and hit him in the forehead. He was startled. He disappeared and came back with an officer. I complained about my shower.

"When your time is up, it's up," said the officer. "You'll have to be punished."

"I know your IRF team. Let them come."

They sprayed me with pepper spray, we fought, and they chained me up. They brought me to solitary confinement. I'd heard of it before, the cell was in Block Oscar.

I looked around. This was truly nothing more than a ship's container with a door. The walls were reinforced by corrugated metal sheeting like the one in fairground stalls. Every surface—the walls, the floor, the ceiling—was covered with it. There was no mattress or wool blanket. A toilet and a sink were sunk into the floor. If I stared for too long at any one point of the metal sheeting, I got dizzy. This cage was even smaller than the one in Block 1.

The light went off. It was cold. The metal on the floor felt like ice. I stood up. Fortunately, I was still wearing my flip-flops, and I hoped the guards wouldn't notice them. I heard a rumbling. It was an air-conditioning unit mounted above the door. Icy air streamed in. I thought back to how I had worked at a bakery when I was young. There was a cooler there, too. I thought, this isn't all that different. They've put me in a giant refrigerator.

After a while, I couldn't feel my hands or legs. I sat down on the floor in a corner of the cell, pulled my pants above my T-shirt and my arms under it all. That was just about bearable. There was a draft. The motor of the air-conditioner was so strong I could feel cold air being sucked in. But I still had no idea what solitary confinement really meant.

There were two slots in the door, one at knee-height for food, and another for the guards to look in. A red light on the ceiling went on when a guard came to bring food or wanted to see me. I think they used it to check whether I was sitting or standing when they pushed through my food. As soon as I took my food, the light went back off, and I ate in the dark. When the guards opened the peephole, I could tell whether it was night or day from whether the light was white or yellow.

Once I succeeded in breaking something in the cell. I kicked the peephole so hard the metal bent a bit and I could see through the crack into the corridor. I shouldn't have done this. When the guards came with my food, I saw them spit on it before they opened the food slot and pushed the plate in. They spat on all the plates before delivering the food. What bastards, I thought. I always looked forward to meals, no matter how scant they were. Now I wasn't able to eat for days. I cleaned every last crumb before I put it in my mouth, and I still felt nauseous.

Sometimes I had to move to fight the cold, but I tried not to. I needed to save my energy since all I was given to eat was a piece of toast and a bit of apple, three times a day. But I had to move around sometimes, when it got colder. I sat in the corner underneath the bare bunk bed. There was no draft there. After a few days, I heard someone speaking Turkish in the corridor. Someone was speaking to one of the guards. I recognized the voice and waited until the guard has gone away.

"Erhan?"

"Murat?"

Erhan was two or three cells down the line from me, but the food slot was open so we could talk to each other when the guards weren't around.

"What are you doing here?" I asked.

"I don't know. And you?"

"I'm vacationing in Siberia."

I got out after a month. For a while, I couldn't see anything. I kept getting terrible headaches. But the sun and the heat were better than the cooler. They brought me to Block Mike in Camp 2. This block, it was said, was completely bugged. Several prisoners had discovered microphones, and we surmised that people were put there so that the soldiers could listen in on their conversations. My neighbor was a man from Saudi Arabia who was married to an American woman. His name was Ebu Ammar.

He was in his mid-thirties and was a taekwondo coach, so I figured I could learn some useful things from him. We talked at night, and he promised to show me a few tricks. From a standing position, he could leap up and touch the ceiling with his foot. We had to be careful because of the guards. Soon I noticed that I was getting increasingly hungry from our secret workouts and the small rations were becoming a problem. But I didn't want to miss the opportunity of having a personal trainer.

I was interrogated in various rooms, and in many of them I noticed cameras in the ventilation shafts. The interrogators varied, too. Every once in a while they were women. Some of them said they could speak German, but most of them couldn't. Over time, I could speak English much better than they could speak German. Through countless interrogations, they always asked the same questions. Hour after hour. When I started to fall asleep from sheer exhaustion, they hit me on the head or in the face. They couldn't think of any better way to keep me awake.

One day, I was taken to an interrogation room in which three women were waiting. The guards chained me to a ring in the floor and left. One of the women was in uniform, but the other two had next to nothing on—just scanty tops and shorts. I looked at the ground. I didn't want to see them, half-naked as they were. One of the women walked around me, put her hand under my shirt from behind and began to stroke me. I like you, she said. I'd like us to do something together.

She said she'd noticed me a while ago and had watched me taking showers. She made some indecent remarks, but I knew she was lying. She couldn't have seen me naked because I always showered in boxer shorts. She pressed her body against mine, stroked my chest and began to moan. It was unbearable. They knew I was religious, and she only wanted to humiliate me. I said: Stop! Stop that! But she kept on. I jerked my head back and caught her on the nose. The door burst open, and the IRF team pounced on me. I was put in the cooler, where I was forced to lie in chains for a whole day and didn't get anything to eat for several more.

Some time later, I was taken to a room with carpeted walls covered with Koranic verses. There was even a prayer rug on the floor. There was a sofa, cushions, a television, and a table on which sat a bowl full of fruit, nuts, and sweets. They had constructed a fantasy paradise. Or I was dreaming. I was starved. But I didn't trust the situation. A man in civilian clothing was sitting on the sofa. He stood up and shook my hand.

"I've heard what happened to you," the man said. "I came immediately from Washington to help you. I'm sorry it took me so long, but the military authorities are slow. They're not allowed to treat you this way. I brought you something to eat. Go ahead and take some."

I remained standing there and said nothing.

"I'm going to help you. But before I can help you, I have to ask you some questions . . ."

"I don't like your food," I said, "or your face."

"You can take it with you to your cell . . ."

"I don't want your food."

"Okay, I can leave you alone. I'll go out, and you can eat. Help yourself . . ."

I didn't touch it.

They had starved me for days. Did they really think they could trick me like this? That I would eat it all up and then tell them what they wanted to hear?

When the escort team brought me back to the cooler, I didn't eat anything for fifteen days in protest. Then my neighbor said, "Murat, that's crazy. You can't go on a hunger strike alone."

He was a Bosnian named Musa. He was right. I started eating again. I was very weak and freezing cold.

They tried every trick in the book. Other prisoners said that they, too, had been humiliated by women. But not all of the female soldiers were like that. Once a female interrogator wanted to shake my hand. I excused myself, looked down, and said I was sorry, explaining that my faith did not allow me to make physical contact with any woman but my wife.

"If you shake hands with a woman, you can get very close to her, and you might begin to feel something for her. It's the first step."

"Why won't you look at me?" asked the woman.

"For the same reason. We aren't allowed to look women in the eye for very long."

"Do you think I'm ugly?"

"It's not that. All women have something beautiful. Probably you're quite lovely."

"What do you do when you meet women on the street? You can't always lower your eyes . . ."

"I'm not responsible for things I can't change," I said. "Only for what I do on purpose."

"If that's the case," she said, "it's okay."

At some point, the interrogations had become so absurd that they were asking me what color shoes I had worn in Bremen or which brand of shirt I preferred. They never stopped interrogating me, so one day I decided not to answer any more questions. For weeks I didn't say a thing, not even "hello." Then an interrogator said:

"Okay, I know you're not answering any questions, but tell me why you've stopped talking."

"I've told you many hundred times what I've done and who I am," I said and pointed to one of the cameras in the room. "If you want to hear my story one more time, you only need to rewind the tapes and play them back."

Of course, they put me in solitary confinement for that. They took away my blanket, my flip-flops, and my T-shirt so that I sat in the cooler in my boxer shorts. But I was always being punished and humiliated, regardless of what I did. The interrogations were especially frequent that autumn. But I said nothing. I only spoke again when the Turks came to Guantanamo.

"Get ready," said the soldier from the escort team, when he came to get me in the morning.

"Where are we going?"

We went to a container I hadn't seen before, located off to the side of the camp. I knew that was where the interrogation rooms for foreign visitors were located. I had heard that other prisoners had been questioned by policemen from their home countries there. What I didn't know was whether I was getting a visit from Germany or Turkey.

There were three men in the interrogation room, and I noticed immediately that they were Turks.

"What's this?" said one of them. "I can't bear to see a Turk bound like this in front of me. That's not right. Call the guard."

No one is more theatrical than the Turks. I couldn't help but smile at the man with the dark hair, who was holding his hand in front of his eyes.

"He's a Turkish citizen, a brother," the man continued. "No, I can't bear to see this. Take his chains off immediately."

The only thing missing were his tears.

The guard came and removed my handcuffs, but he left the foot restraints chained to the ring in the floor. What nonsense! Great show, I thought, but this is still just one big set-up. The Turk came up to me, shook my hand, and then kissed me on the cheeks.

"How do you feel? How are you doing? I can't believe my eyes."

The man then collected himself and sat down. He didn't introduce himself. He told the other two men to be quiet, although they hadn't said anything, and then said he would have to ask me a few questions. He wanted to know where I had been arrested.

"In Pakistan," I said. "I wasn't exactly arrested. I was asked to get out of the bus and answer some questions, so I got out."

The Turk's tone of voice changed instantaneously.

"What sort of lies are you telling?" he yelled. "We spare no expense and effort to come here, and you start lying? If you don't want us to help you, that's your decision. Why did you decide to become a terrorist?"

"I'm not a terrorist."

"Oh no? Then what are you? If you weren't a terrorist, you wouldn't have ended up here. You're all terrorists in here."

The man stood up and threatened me with his fist. But I wasn't afraid. On the contrary. I was enraged.

"Have you come here to help or shower me with stupid insults?" I asked.

"We don't give a shit if you spend the rest of your life in Guantanamo. We want to ask our questions and leave. America will decide the rest. We don't have any influence on that."

The other two men still hadn't said a word.

From the way the man talked, I got the impression that he didn't know exactly where he was. I told him about the cells and torture in Guantanamo and Kandahar. The three men listened to me for a while, before their leader hastily interrupted.

"What are you thinking? Do you believe you'd be treated any better in a Turkish prison?" I knew then that he truly didn't care.

They asked me a few meaningless questions, which I answered, although I found them a waste of time.

The next morning I was brought into a room where the Americans usually interrogated me. It was one of the spaces with a one-way mirror behind the lectern. The three Turks were there again. This time they did-n't say hello, and there wasn't any show. They asked me some questions about my German friends in Bremen. They seemed especially interested in two of my friends who worked for the Bremen police department.

"How come you had friends who worked for the police?"

"I don't understand the question," I said. "They're my friends. They just happen to work for the police. One of them is Turkish, the other German . . . I don't know. That's just the way it turned out . . ."

"You're lying. We're convinced that you're a spy. That's the evidence. You're a German spy."

That was absurd. What sort of a spy was I supposed to be? One who spied on Guantanamo? Who would voluntarily let himself be imprisoned here to spy for Germany? Or a spy in Bremen who kept the Turks in Hemelingen under surveillance? What was the point of this? I was fed up.

"Okay, if you think I'm a spy, then that's it. I don't know what you're talking about, but if you want to think I'm a spy, go ahead."

"We have some more questions . . ."

"I'm not answering any more questions."

For a while they kept trying to get answers, but I was fed up. I knew these kind of people, and the Turkish government wasn't going to help me. Not in a million years.

"Well, that's all." said the leader of the three men. "You deserve to be here."

The Turk and his two subordinates left.

I'd already regretted talking to them during the first interrogation, and I had given up hope they would believe me. Even the Americans didn't think I was a spy. They probably had a good laugh behind the mirror when they heard that.

A little while later, the Germans came. It was September 23, 2002.

Strangely enough, the night before, I got a new neighbor in Block Mike, the one that was bugged. He was a large man. They put him in the cage opposite mine. I talked to him. His name was Abid—I can't remem-ber his last name, although I could see the band around his wrist.

"Where are you from?" I asked.

"Germany," he said.

"Germany?"

I was amazed. I thought I was the only prisoner from Germany. Abid was over 40. He was originally Algerian, and he said that he had lived in Hamburg for a number of years and was married to a German woman. He'd worked there as a bouncer in a club. Abid had been in prison a number of times before. He told me about jails in Algeria, France, and Italy, and he said that when he was bouncer he had done some time in a Hamburg prison after a fight. But he'd never experienced anything like Guantanamo, he said. His German was very good, and when he stood up, I saw that he had a limp.

The next day when I entered the room where the three Turks had interrogated me, there was a man sitting at the table. They chained my foot restraints to the ring on the floor. Then three other men came in. They must be Germans, I thought. They didn't look like Turks. Two of them were wearing suits, while the other two wore casual shirts and pants. One of them was blond and had a moustache and a goatee. He was big and strong. One of them was thin and also had a moustache, while the third had a receding hairline. The fourth left the room after a while without having said anything. I couldn't tell whether he was German or American.

One of the men put a cassette recorder on the table. It was pleasantly cool—there had to be an air conditioner on somewhere. The big guy, who had already been sitting in the room when I entered, seemed younger than the other two.

"We're from Germany, and we want to ask you some questions."

There was no greeting and none of the men introduced himself, but I said that I was glad to finally speak to someone from the German government. They asked me how I was doing. I said that I was always hungry, that it was very hot, that the cells were too small, and that we were hardly ever let out in the yard. They didn't seem too interested.

"If you answer the questions truthfully, you'll help yourself. Start with your life story."

"Have you brought me anything from Germany?" I asked. "A letter or a message from my family?"

They looked at one another and shrugged.

"We've come here to ask questions, not to deliver letters."

I notice that the blond one stayed in the background. The other two seemed to be in charge.

"Why don't you begin . . ."

I told them about everything. About the discos, my bodybuilding, my friends in Hemelingen, and my visits to the mosques. They seemed especially interested in how and why I had become religious. They kept interrupting my answers with other questions.

"How important is that to you?"

"Do feel superior to other people?"

"Do you hate non-religious Muslims?"

"Do you hate Germans because they're not religious?"

"Which people, if any, mean anything to you?"

They took turns. After a while they called to a guard who took off my handcuffs. The fourth man entered the room every once in a while and whispered to the others.

I told them about my family, my friends, and Selcuk. They wanted to know what plans Selcuk had, whether I thought he was dangerous, and whether I could imagine him as a criminal. No, I said, I couldn't. I told them about the *tablighis*, and they named some people from the group in Bremen. They asked if these were common names. They showed me some photos that I hadn't seen before in the interrogations with the Americans. Pictures of friends and colleagues from work, from my apprenticeship, and the trade school. They also showed me photos of girls, but I didn't know any of them. They showed me pictures of men in mosques and on the street, but I didn't know most of them either. Then they showed me pictures of Selcuk. One of them showed him laughing.

"Why is he laughing?" I asked.

"Yes, he's doing well," said the blond man. "Unlike you."

The other two left the room. As they shut the door, the clock fell off the wall and revealed a camera pepping out a hole. The big blonde guy picked up the clock and hung it back up. I could see the camera lens above the number 3. The other two men returned.

"If you answer our questions truthfully, it may speed up your release."

That was the same thing the Americans said, but the Germans seemed more professional. They knew everything about me, and suddenly they read out a sentence that left me amazed.

"Selcuk went with a friend to Afghanistan to fight there. He was stirred up to do so in a mosque . . ."

Allegedly Selcuk's brother had told a customs official this on the telephone at Frankfurt Airport. Selcuk, the Germans said, had received a fine because his dog had bitten someone. He hadn't paid it, and when he went with the officials into their office and called his brother, the brother had refused to help him and told the officials not to let him leave under any circumstances. I don't know whether this was true. But I could imagine it was.

Now I knew why Selcuk hadn't come to Pakistan and why the Americans in Kandahar already knew so much about me. The customs official must have passed on the information, and it had gotten to the Americans. I told the Germans I didn't know anything about this phone call because at that point I was already on the plane.

"I think he probably didn't want to let Selcuk go, just as my mother or brother wouldn't have let me go. I don't know why he said that, but I imagine he made it up. He wanted to prevent Selcuk and me from flying to Pakistan. He probably didn't know I was already on the plane at that point and that he could get me in trouble. My parents or my brother might have made up something similar to keep me from going."

The Germans said two students at my trade school had testified that I ran around the school with a big turban and had said I wanted to become a Taliban fighter. They showed me pictures of two students. They were both Turks.

Those were the same two people, I said, who used to accuse me of being a pimp. When I was eighteen, I used to drive my father's Mercedes to the trade school on Thursdays and Fridays. Back then, I worked in discos, had short hair, shaved, and wore stylish suits. The two Turks had always tried to get me into trouble. Where did he get the Mercedes? they'd ask. He's definitely dealing drugs. That was a lie, and now they were telling more lies about me. I never said I wanted to become a Taliban fighter or go to war in any form. And I never wore a turban.

"You bought combat boots, fatigues, and field glasses before you flew to Pakistan . . ."

Combat boots? Did they mean the pair of KangaROOS that the police in Pakistan had taken from me? Fatigues? In Bremen, I had bought a pair of pants with side pockets and removable legs that you can get in any camping store.

"And as far as the field glasses were concerned," I said, "I did have a simple pair of binoculars with me, but they were small enough to fit in my shirt pocket. My parents gave them to me. Now they're gone."

I had a pain in my elbow and kept massaging that spot. One of the Germans asked why I kept doing that. I told him about the IRF teams, and explained that one of the soldiers had twisted my arm.

"But that's nothing," I said, and told them about being tortured in Kandahar, about the electric shocks and chains, the water-boarding and solitary confinement cells in Guantanamo, even about the incident with the women.

None of that seemed to interest them.

"Let's get back to the point," they said every time I told them about being tortured.

That evening I was back in Block Mike.

"How was it?" asked Ebu Ammar.

"I had visitors."

"Germans?"

"Yes."

"Germans are known to be just. You've got no worries. If they've come all the way over here to interrogate you, they'll bring you back to Germany soon."

"The Germans will probably interrogate me as well," said Abid.

Definitely, I thought, he was from Germany, too.

That night I thought about what the visit might mean. The Germans hadn't exactly been helpful and had tried to trick me, and when I'd asked them whether I had been given a lawyer in Germany and whether people there had any information about me, they had just said they weren't able to answer those questions.

Like the Americans, they had only been after evidence they could use to accuse me of some crime.

Whenever I spoke about being tortured, they changed the subject. But the truth was I had been tortured! I had to tell them! As interrogators, they were duty-bound to carefully record everything I said and to make it known to my family, the German government, and the public. Weren't they supposed to have asked me about my treatment as well? But at least, I thought, our conversation had been taped.

I was convinced that my family and the German public knew that government representatives had come to see me. Surely it was an official visit.

The next day I told them about Abid from Hamburg, my neighbor in Block Mike. Who was that, they wanted to know, and I told them what I knew about him.

They asked whether I knew him from Germany.

"No," I said. "The Americans call him the 'Big German Guy.'"

But my German interrogators didn't seem interested in Abid.

They came and went from the room again, as they had the day before. Maybe they wanted to talk something over in private, or perhaps they had just smoked a cigarette.

"We have a number of questions we want you to answer only with a simple yes or no. You should answer immediately without taking time to think. Just yes or no. Is that clear?"

"Okay."

"Have you ever worn black shoes?"

"Yes."

"Have you ever seen children's films?"

"Yes."

"Are you from Al Qaeda?"

"No."

Trick questions, I thought.

"Faster," they said. "You have to answer faster. Do you drink water?"

"Yes."

"Have you ever had a toothache?"

"Yes."

"Do you love your mother?"

"Yes."

"Did you want to join the Taliban?"

"No."

"Do you like your father?"

"Yes."

"Did Selcuk pay for your ticket?

"No."

"Have you ever had a pet?"

"Yes."

"Have you ever experimented with explosives?"

"No."

"Do you approve of Osama bin Laden?"

"No."

"Do you like your brother?"

"Yes."

"Do you like Osama?"

This went on for at least an hour.

The big blond guy didn't say much during this, and then the other two left the room, leaving him behind alone. When they came back, they wanted to know what I intended to do after I was released. Did I want to get a job?

"Of course, I want to work," I said. "How else am I going to earn money?"

"Would you like to work for us when you return to Germany?"

I thought it over. "What would I do for you?"

"Find out interesting things. You would get into certain circles to which others don't have access."

"What kind of circles? The Hell's Angels?"

I had to laugh. Of course I knew they were talking about mosques and the *tablighis*.

"You could be a big help to us . . ."

They wanted me to spy for them. I would never do that, I thought. I'd rather starve to death. But it might help me to feign interest.

"What would it be like?"

"We'll tell you as things progress. But we have a V-man who would meet you daily at prearranged times and places."

I nodded. At the time, I didn't know that a V-man was the German term for an undercover informant, so I would have nodded just the same if he had said X-man or T-man.

"Okay," I said. "Good idea. Let's do it. Will I contact you?"

"No. You can meet the V-man whenever you want. He'll pass on everything you have to us."

Then all three of them left the room. After a while they came back.

"Mr. Kurnaz," they said. "We believe you've lied to us. There are some things we want to check to get concrete evidence against you. You'll see. It looks very bad for you."

"But why?" I cried. "I told you everything. You know that. You know everything about me."

"We have our own evidence. We'll base our actions on that."

"You know all too well that I have nothing to do with any terrorists."

"That's it then. We're going back to Germany."

They left the room, and the escort team came and brought me back to Block Mike.

"You see," said Abid, "they only came because of you. If they were interested in holding interrogations, they would have questioned me, too. But they only wanted to talk to you. You'll be home soon."

Home soon? Before I was captured, I never could have imagined a government like Germany's covering up the fact that it had sent intelligence agents to visit someone like me, but now I wasn't so sure. After all, they had suggested that I become a spy for them in Bremen.

The Germans interrogated me for around twelve hours those two days, and afterward Abid was transferred, and the Americans intensified their questioning. I was interrogated two or three times a day. They desperately wanted to know what the Germans had asked me and what I had told them. Why did you tell them about being tortured? they asked, pulling my hair. You're only making things worse for yourself. For days, they asked nothing but questions about what I'd told the Germans, even though they already knew what I'd said. What lies did I tell them, the Americans asked. They also asked me about the "Big German Guy." But what was I supposed to tell them about him?

Later I found out there were another two prisoners from Germany. One was a Tunisian, the other an Algerian. The Algerian, whose brother lives in Frankfurt, gave me his address in case I was ever released. But I don't have the address any more. It was taken away from me during the next cell search.

In late 2002, General Geoffrey Miller took over command of Guantanamo, and our situation dramatically worsened. The interrogations got more brutal, more frequent, and longer. The first order General Miller issued was to commence Operation Sandman, which meant we were moved to new cells every one or two hours. The general's goal was to completely deprive us of sleep, and he achieved it.

I was moved from one block to the next. The escort team would storm in, put me in chains, run with me through the corridors, push me to my knees, and leave me there. The whole procedure would be repeated an hour later. I was transferred from Camp 1, Block Alpha, to Camp 2, Block Echo or from Camp 1, Block Alpha, to Camp 2, Block Bravo. The chains were put on and removed. I had to stand and kneel—twenty-four hours a day. I had barely arrived in a new cell and lay down on the bunk, before they came again to move me.

My neighbors were perplexed because not all the prisoners were treated this way. Later I found out that the operation was carried out on five specially selected prisoners. I was among the first—perhaps because I had refused to confess.

When the escort team had finally left the cell, I'd say hello to my neighbors, sit or lie on the bunk, and try to sleep. But as soon as the guards saw me close my eyes, sitting or lying on the bunk, they'd kick the door and yell at me, until I got up again. Soon I didn't bother greeting my neighbors. I just fell down on the bunk and tried to get a moment's sleep, before the guards woke me with a kick at the door or a punch in the face. There were maybe ten or fifteen minutes a day when I wasn't being watched.

In between transfers, I was interrogated. During this period, my interrogator was always the same man and the questioning went on a lot longer; I estimated the sessions lasted up to fifteen hours. During the sessions, the man would simply disappear for hours. I sat chained to my chair or kneeling on the floor, and as soon as my eyelids drooped, soldiers would wake me with a couple of blows. Once I spent more than two days in the interrogation room before the man returned.

The man told me to call him Jack (not his real name). He asked whether I wanted to change my story.

"If you change your story," Jack said, "I'll be able to help you."

Cage door open, cage door closed. Standing, kneeling, standing, kneeling. The escort team came, the escort team went.

"Do you want to tell me something interesting?" asked Jack. "If you do, I can get you a nice place to sleep. Nice and warm with a mattress and a blanket."

Days and nights without sleep. Blows and new cages. Again, the stabbing sensation of a thousand needles throughout my entire body. I would have loved to step outside my body, but I couldn't.

"If you work with me," Jack said, "you can sleep for as long as you want."

I no longer knew what block I was in. Sometimes, I would start quivering for no reason. The movement of my hands, arms, and legs seemed to be taking place in a dream.

"I've gotten used to the metal bunks," I told Jack.

Sometimes I heard ringing sounds that weren't there. Other times I heard a low hum in my ear that refused to go away.

"You can keep your bed, Jack!"

"Okay," said Jack. "If you think this is fun, keep it up."

When I could no longer get up, they sent the IRF team, who said they would hit me for as long as it took for me to get up and go with them to the next cell. But I was too weak. All I could feel was a buzzing in my head like a siren. They picked me up, and my knees buckled. During the last days of this treatment, they had to carry me around. They'd take me from one cage to the next, then to Jack, and then to another cage. I can only remember bits and pieces of this.

In the end they gave up—probably because it was simply too much work for the guards to carry me around all the time. Over time, it was as if they were the ones getting punished. I was allowed to sleep, and when I woke up, the other prisoners helped me calculate how long this treatment had lasted. Three weeks. I went three weeks without sleep. At this point, I weighed less than 130 pounds.

———————————

The air-conditioning units in the solitary confinement cells varied between cold and hot, so when they brought me to solitary confinement,

I didn't know whether I would freeze or sweat. In the next few years, I was transferred back and forth between Camps 1 and 2 within Camp Delta. In total, I estimate I spent around eighteen months in Camp 1 and maybe two years in Camp 2. The rest of the time I spent in the isolation blocks Oscar, November, and India as well as Romeo and Quebec, whose walls were covered in Plexiglas.

Those cells were like ovens. The sun beat down on the metal roof at noon and directly on the sides of the cage in the mornings and afternoons. All told, I think I spent roughly a year alone in absolute darkness, either in a cooler or an oven, with little food, and once I spent three months straight in solitary confinement.

The rules for solitary confinement changed every few months. Sometimes I was allowed a blanket at night and then would have to hand it over in the morning. Sometimes I didn't get a blanket at all. Sometimes there was a mattress, sometimes not. During one stint I got food, and none the next.

The procedure with blankets worked like this. The guard would appear in the morning, and I would shove it, folded, through the slot. One time the guard called the IRF team and told them I had refused to hand over my blanket so they stormed into the cell and beat me up. They especially liked doing this to me after I had broiled in an oven and froze in a cooler for a month. They'd then say I had broken the rules and extend my term of solitary confinement for another four weeks.

I couldn't see any point to what they were doing. They could have just locked me up in solitary confinement for months on end if they wanted to. Why the pretense? It was up to individual interrogators anyway to determine how long they kept me and other prisoners in isolation. When an interrogator told the guards after questioning that I would have to stay in solitary confinement for another four weeks, that's what happened. I would be put back in the hole, and every time I was due to be released, they'd say I refused to hand over my blanket or spit on the ground or insulted a guard, and I'd get four more weeks of solitary confinement. The only law was my captors themselves, regardless of what they wrote in the forms they were constantly filling out.

At some point, it occurred to me that they were probably just writing down excuses in their reports. That I had gotten a blanket and refused to give it back. That a punishment had been ordered because I had clearly violated the rules. That the IRF team had to be called to bring the prisoner to reason. That I would have to spend a further month in solitary confinement in accordance with the rules. Everything was crystal clear. What could they do about it? The prisoner should have handed over his blanket. That's the way it would look to an outsider, I thought as I sat in the dark and the heat or the cold, should an outsider ever read these documents. That hypothetical someone would never imagine the guards were lying.

That just about drove me crazy, and the more I thought about it, the angrier I became. I didn't think the guards were acting on their own accord, just to be evil. People higher up had drawn up regulations so that they could one day say that there had been rules, clear and fair, but no one would ever find out about the one overarching, unspoken rule that mandated that the rest of the regulations were to be constantly broken. On paper, I would always be the one who had broken the rules. I thought a lot about this in the darkness.

They had robbed me of my freedom. They had taken away part of my youth, valuable time, probably the most important time in my life. They had taken my family, my passport, and my rights. They had robbed me of sun and sleep and put me in coolers and ovens. If we had been able to survive without food, they would have taken that away, too. They only gave us enough to survive. The only thing I still had was the air I breathed. At least they couldn't take that away, I thought, this air, which stank of rust and diesel fuel.

But once again, I was mistaken.

It was my time to go into the rec area for a walk, and two soldiers, one black and one white, escorted me there. I had just walked into the yard, but after I had taken only four or five steps, the white soldier shouted:

"Come back out of there! Come on, out! Back in your cage!"

"Why? I just got here!"

"Time's up," said the white soldier smiling. "I'm the one making the decisions around here, and I say you're going back into your cage now."

"OK," I said.

Then they chained me up. Once I was back in the cell, it wasn't long before the white soldier reappeared.

"Do you want to take a shower?" he asked.

Maybe he wants to make it up to me, I thought.

"OK, you can shower," he said.

They led me to the shower cell and unchained me, but it was just the same harassment. The white soldier turned on the water as I was getting undressed, and as soon as I wanted to get into the shower, he turned it off again.

"Time's up," he said.

The guards both laughed.

"You're going back home."

"OK. I'm going back to the cage. But this cage is nothing. What do you think your cage will look like in hell?"

"I don't believe in that kind of nonsense," said the white guard. "Shut up!"

They chained me up again and we walked along the corridor. The other prisoners were praying, so the guard began to whistle and stomped with his boots on the arched parts of the metal flooring, making it bang. Then he started to run very quickly, pulling me behind him on the chain like a mule and jerking me back and forth on the shackles. The black guard was behind me. Finally, I lost my temper.

I stopped.

"Keep moving!"

"Stop jerking me back and forward like that."

"Move!"

He wrenched me back and forward again.

That was it.

Although my hands were chained together in front of my stomach, I managed to grab his hand, then his sleeve, and his shoulder. My wrists were bleeding, but I didn't care. I wanted to show him that I could get the better of him—with or without handcuffs. I already had him by the collar, and he tried a judo move, shoving his leg in front of my hip to throw me. But I leapt over his leg with my chained feet and threw him over my hip so that he landed on his back. I had taken him down with his own trick. I jumped on top of him and brought my forehead crashing down on his nose. It started bleeding immediately, and the soldier groaned. I kneed him in the ribs.

It had all happened very quickly. The black guard tore at my hair, but he couldn't pull me off the soldier. He kicked my head and my back, but I didn't stop. The guard ran off.

When he came back, I heard the voice of the block sergeant.

"Stop! Stop it! Let go of him!"

"OK," I said, "But first you have to promise he'll keep his mouth shut. Then I'll let him go."

"I promise," said the sergeant.

I let the soldier go.

No sooner was he back on his feet then he pulled me to the ground and sat on top of me. The sergeant and the other soldiers restrained my feet and hands and pressed my shoulders and my head to the floor.

Someone shouted, "They're finishing off Murat!"

The prisoners shouted and kicked their doors.

"It's alright," I shouted. "I'm alright."

The prisoners in the block calmed down again. The guards stuck me in my cell. The soldier whose nose was bleeding locked the door.

"You're not a man!" I said. "You're just a load of hot air. I beat you up when I was in handcuffs and shackles."

"You didn't beat me up. There's no way you could beat me up!"

"So what did I just do?"

I washed my hands and feet and tried to clean the blood off my T-shirt and pants. Then I got ready for prayers. I bowed down and began, although I knew what was coming.

The IRF team pulled me out of the cell, down the corridor, and out into the open. There they waited for the papers that would permit them to take me to solitary confinement. They threw me to the ground, surrounding me.

"This is how we do it here," said the soldier whose nose was still red.

"That still doesn't make you a man," I replied.

I didn't feel much after that. They dragged me semiconscious to block India.

It was the first day of fasting the month of Ramadan, Winter 2003.

I was put in a solitary confinement cell like any other, fitted out with corrugated metal sheeting. I had never been to India, and I was surprised that it wasn't cold. I immediately realized that something was wrong. There wasn't any air! The air conditioning unit over the door wasn't humming, and that was the only supply of air in here. They had turned off the air conditioning.

I kicked the peephole to move it a bit. I kicked it again and again but nothing happened. Had I become too weak, or was the peephole just built better than in the other cells? After several attempts I gave up. The effort was costing me too much oxygen. The walls were covered in condensation. It was hot.

I kicked the side of the cell to see if I had a neighbor. I held my ear close to one place where the welding looked weak. I already knew that we would have to speak quietly, or else they would spray pepper gas into the cell. I had been completely alone in solitary confinement often enough—without any neighbors to talk to.

"*Salaam alaikum*," I said.

There was no answer. I kicked the wall again.

"*Salaam alaikum?*"

"*Alaikum salam!* Who is it?"

"It's me, Murat!"

"Which Murat?"

"Turkish Murat! From Germany . . ."

"Long time no hear! How are you?"

I recognized the voice. It was the man I had seen in X-Ray. The man who weighed less than ninety pounds and was waiting to die.

"Is it you, Daoud? Abu Daoud?"

"Yes . . ."

Suddenly the peephole opened. Tear gas streamed into my cell.

"Quiet! You're not allowed to talk!"

The gas stung my eyes, but I was curious. I was happy he was still alive, and wanted to know if he had put on weight, although I couldn't speak because I had to cough and couldn't catch my breath. I couldn't say anything for several hours. Whenever I tried, I started coughing and gasping for air. I drank some water, water that stank of chlorine—but it didn't help. The gas didn't disperse. The cell must have been completely insulated. I heard Daoud knocking every half an hour and saying:

"Murat! Murat? Are you still there?"

The peephole opened again. Nothing happened. They just wanted to see what I was doing. Some fresh air came in that way and I felt better afterward. After a while I tried to speak to Daoud again. Very quietly. I knew I couldn't survive another round of tear gas. I would have suffocated. I knocked on the wall.

"Murat? Are you there?"

Abu Daoud had in fact put on weight. I was pleased to hear that he was feeling better, but I couldn't talk any more. I had to cough again, and I didn't have the energy to stay on my feet or to speak. I lay down on the bunk, but after a while I was hardly getting any air so I moved to the floor. Maybe it would be better there. But I was too tired to even sit up straight. I lay down on my back and pressed my nose up close to the crack between the floor and the wall, thinking that some air must have been coming through there since the crack wasn't sealed with rubber. I breathed very slowly, but it was becoming tortuous, as if whatever air I did manage to catch was becoming heavier and heavier. I felt dizzy.

I don't know if I blacked out at some point. Maybe I fell asleep. Maybe I lost consciousness. A number of times I could sense myself waking back up, and then the guards kicked the door and opened the peephole.

That let some air in. I opened my eyes.

"Yes, he's still alive," one of the soldiers said.

"OK, then close up again," said the other.

I lay back down on the cell floor until they returned—it took hours. This time I had decided not to open my eyes so that some more air could come into the cell through the peephole. It opened.

"India 2! Wake up!"

They kicked the door, and then I heard the guards close the flap and disappear. Footsteps from several guards followed. The flap opened again, but I kept my eyes closed.

"Wake up!"

They sprayed me with water from a high-pressure hose, which felt like a slap in the face, the water getting into my nose and mouth. I jumped up. I no longer cared about air. The hose was stuck through the peephole, and I heard the guards laughing as I fell over. The stream of water forced me back against the wall. Then it was over and the guards moved off, laughing. The floor was covered with water. I lay down on the bunk, but I couldn't get any air so I lay back down on the wet floor. I could breathe a bit better there. The water slowly drained away.

It was Ramadan, and I was given a slice of white bread and a few small carrots or a quarter of an apple in the evening. Once I was given a quarter of a pear. That made me think about how we used to stuff ourselves in the evenings at home during Ramadan. I was getting less and less air. I blacked out.

I woke up when the guards came. The flap opened, the red light went on, and some air came in. Sometimes I got up to pray, but I didn't know whether the time was right. Thoughts whirred through my head, most of them about food. I remembered eating whole packets of sliced bread with cold cuts and cheese for breakfast. Now I was getting one slice three times a day. I thought about my family who were celebrating Ramadan right now in Hemelingen. What would my mother be serving for breakfast?

I blacked out. The flap opened. I opened my eyes and realized that I needed air more desperately than food or water to survive.

Air, just air.

On the third day of Eid, after Ramadan, they finally opened the door and let me out.

It was evening. The prisoners in Camp 1 were singing Islamic songs. The guards kicked the doors and ordered them to stop, but they kept on singing. I met the guard whom I had beaten up in the corridor. He was wearing sunglasses and pretended not to pay me any attention. On my way to the cage, the prisoners greeted me.

"Where were you?"

"Solitary confinement."

"Which block?"

"India."

"The whole of Ramadan?"

I had been in India 2 for thirty-three days.

———————————

They had fine-tuned the Guantanamo system. I understood now that prisoners were intended to feel as miserable and desperate as possible every single moment of their lives—this, as the Americans would say, was "maximum discomfort." They were constantly depriving me of anything that would have helped me get used to my situation: sleep, a blanket, time, exercise, food, air.

I would only just start to get adjusted to my new neighbors when I was taken to another cage or put into solitary confinement. They put us under maximum pressure around the clock, separating us from anything that could have given us strength or confidence. That's why we were continually moved and questioned. They ridiculed our faith and tried to separate us from Allah to make us give up any hope of ever getting out of that hell. We were to be made as weak and as small as possible so they could get something out of us in interrogation or at least break us. I didn't give up hope. It is part of my faith never to give up hope. If Allah was willing, I could be released at any moment.

One day I was taken back to the container that was reserved for use by foreign interrogators. The big, blond German guy was sitting at the table. The other two hadn't come. An American was sitting next to the German, who had put his feet up on the table and was staring at the screen of a laptop. There were motorbike magazines lying next to it. I was happy. He'd brought them, I thought, because last time I had told him that I liked motorcycles. I was shackled to the chair. The German didn't acknowledge my presence but just showed the American something on the screen. They whispered to each other.

That lasted about two hours. I sat in the chair and waited. They didn't say a word to me, and the magazines were too far away for me to see them. Suddenly the German lifted his head and stared at me.

"It's been almost two years, Mr. Kurnaz, and today you had another chance to prove to me that you are innocent. But you messed it up. Unfortunately, you didn't use your time."

"I thought you were going to ask me questions?"

"That was very clever of you. Today your time is up, but tomorrow you'll get one last chance. I don't have much time, so think hard about what you are going to say."

Then he disappeared.

The next morning I was brought back into the room, where the big, blond German guy was sitting at the desk. He pushed a CD into his laptop without saying a word. Photos of Selcuk, obviously taken surreptitiously, appeared on the screen. In one of them, Selcuk was praying in a mosque. The picture was taken from the floor. Maybe with a watch or a mobile phone, I thought. In another picture, Selcuk was sitting in front of his balcony door in his undershirt, yawning. In a third, he was talking to young people, and in others, he was entering or leaving a mosque.

"Do you still think you want to work with us?"

"Yes," I said.

"OK. We will let you know. It will probably work out. But you will have to cooperate and tell all."

He pressed a button and shut down the computer. Then he put his feet on the table and leaned back, his hands clasped behind his head.

"You have nothing to worry about. After all, you're on a Caribbean island. Relax."

He closed the laptop, stood up, and went to the door. Then he turned around.

"Have a look at the biker magazines, if you want."

I glanced at them. They were from April 2004.

Sometimes iguanas came into the blocks. One of them crawled up the lattice of my cage, and I fed it breadcrumbs. It ate out of my hand and slept in a pipe above my cage. I saw it crawling out of it in the morning. Sometimes land crabs came out of the pipe, tiny ones. They also liked bread. Once, a guard caught me feeding the iguana. That meant ten days in solitary confinement—the most lenient punishment there was.

When I heard wild screams again, I knew it could only be something involving the Koran. One of the guards had taken a Koran, thrown it onto the floor, and trampled it. We could only hear the wailing from a far-off block, but we knew what had happened. That same evening, a prisoner ripped up his T-shirt and tried to hang himself.

I could hear the IRF teams and the guards nervously walking back and forth. There was tear gas in the air. The prisoner was immediately discovered and taken away. Several people had threatened to commit suicide if the Koran was desecrated again, and that's how the new hunger strike began. The news was passed on from block to block. We knew almost everyone would take part.

I didn't eat anything for twenty days. The last two or three days I didn't drink any water either. It simply became too strenuous for me to use the tap. You had to press it down really hard. I tried to walk the few paces that were possible in the cell, but at some point, I didn't have enough strength. Starving myself was becoming increasingly difficult because some of my neighbors in the blocks had started eating again. I could smell the food, even when it was cold or lukewarm. I battled with myself, but decided to see my hunger strike through. My faith didn't prescribe it, I just wanted the desecration of the Holy Book to stop. Meanwhile, the interrogations continued.

I was getting weaker and weaker, and at some point they came, put me on a stretcher, and took me to a medical ward. I clung to the stretcher. My whole body cramped up—I was afraid they would amputate one of my limbs. Two men appeared, in uniform, and one had a badge on his chest with the word Doctor. That really frightened me.

"Do you want to eat now, or not?" asked the doctor.

"No."

They gagged me and shoved a tube up my nose, stopping several times because the tube filled with blood. Then I was taken to interrogation. An IRF team beat me, while I was still lying on the stretcher.

Eventually, I was taken back to the block, where I was told that one of the emirs had arranged with the general for all copies of the Koran to be taken out of the cells. Some of the prisoners were already in critical condition because of the hunger strike. The Americans probably thought it would be too much work keeping us alive with those tubes. The emir had negotiated the deal, and the general's suggestions were discussed in each block. All except three or four of the prisoners started eating again after that. The second condition of the deal was that they would no longer play the American national anthem during our prayers. A third condition was that we would receive hot meals. After the hunger strike was over, they presented us with a menu that listed very exotic dishes: Thai chicken, lamb curry, or Turkish pasha rolls. But when we got our first platefuls, we saw the same things as always: vegetables and bread, mashed together, or half-cooked rice with pieces of fruit. If "Mediterranean chicken breast" was written on the menu, then there would be a couple of hard potatoes and two tough strips of dried-out chicken on our plates.

I started eating again for two days, but then I couldn't stomach anything. Whenever I went to the bathroom, I had blood in my urine. My whole body ached and I was running a high fever. I could hardly move—even talking was too tiring. My neighbor told the guards that I wasn't well. It was Nuri, the electrician from Izmir, who I hadn't seen for years.

"Nuri, I don't want to go to the infirmary. Don't tell them to take me there."

"Murat, you have to let them treat you."

"So they can amputate something? No! Don't tell them anything. I'm staying here!"

When the guards came, Nuri told them that I was still weak after the hunger strike and was asleep. On the second or third day of fever, I didn't get up at all. I tried to say something to Nuri, but I couldn't. I couldn't even turn my head.

I sensed that I was going to die.

"Murat? Can you still hear me?"

Late at night he called out to me again.

"Murat . . ."

I didn't have the strength to say very much.

"Listen. There's no point any more. If you get out, tell my family how I died."

Nuri beat his fist against the mesh. He was crying.

Then it went quiet.

I still don't know what was wrong with me. Perhaps, because of my hunger strike, my body couldn't get rid of waste. I had hardly gone to the toilet during that whole time, and maybe my body had been poisoned. Or perhaps it simply couldn't take food any longer. I must have laid in my

cell for several days. I remember occasionally opening my eyes and looking at the ceiling. I couldn't tell if it was day or night. I don't remember
any more.

I woke up on a stretcher in a medical ward.

A bottle of transparent liquid was hanging above me, and there was a
needle in my arm. I was weak and in pain. I couldn't see anyone, only a
machine that beeped. My hands and feet were in chains, but they were
still there. I was relieved. At some point they removed the tubes.
Someone asked me some questions. Whether I had been sick as a child.
What illnesses I'd had.

I could sit up. I could eat. I had survived.

I could even hear music.

The guards were listening to rock music.

Every prisoner knew who General Miller was and what we had to thank
him for when Operation Sandman commenced and harsher interrogations and confinements were introduced. The general often strode
through the blocks together with a group of officers, grinning as if he was
very pleased. He was an older man, tall and a bit paunchy. He walked
around in a uniform with lots of stars on his shoulders, handing out coins
to the guards and block sergeants. One of the sergeants was so happy
that he even showed the coin to some of the prisoners. I called out and
asked him whether I could see it, too.

"A coin from the general!" he said. "He gave me it because I'm good."

"Really? From General Miller?"

"Yes," he said and opened the flap.

He pressed the coin into my hand. The name of the general, Geoffrey
Miller, was written on it. Underneath: Guantanamo. There were stars on
it and a motto, something like: "General Miller is helping make the world
a better place."

I took the coin, threw it in the toilet, and flushed.

"What are you doing?" shouted the sergeant.

He ran straight out and came back with an IRF team. After they were finished with me, they reached into the toilet U-bend and tried to fish out the coin. It was gone. Of course, I was sent to solitary confinement.

I had been sitting on my bunk for several days before I noticed that the guards had left the peepholes open so that they could simply look in as they passed by. I heard steps in the corridor and pressing my eye to my peephole, I saw that they were all open. I heard one of the prisoners shouting in Arabic: "Listen up, Miller's coming! If you want to give him a gift, then get ready and do it now!" The flaps were open because of Miller's visit.

This was an order, and I knew what was going to happen. General Miller had come to inspect Oscar Block. Another general or high-ranking officer and several captains were walking by his side.

When they reached the middle of the corridor, the first prisoner threw a mixture of water and feces, collected in a bowl or in an Emarie packet, at the general. He hit his target. The general let out a cry, held up his arms to shield his face and turned away. At that moment, he got another load from the cell opposite. He ran down the corridor to the end of the block, and everyone else hurled the contents of his bowl. The officers tried to shield the general. The captain, who placed himself between us and the general, was spared.

Our punishment turned out to be relatively mild. We were not given any bread for several days, and our spell in solitary confinement was extended by a month. There was nothing else they could have done short of killing us.

A few weeks, later I saw Miller in a Camp 1 block. He was strutting through the corridor as usual.

"Why are you walking about so arrogantly? Everyone knows that you ate shit in Oscar," one prisoner said in perfect English.

Miller turned red and started walking more quickly.

"Your name is Miller? We've got a better name for you: Mr. Toilet!"

The prisoners laughed. That day there was no food for the whole block and rations were halved for about forty days.

But from then on, General Miller was known by his new name among the prisoners.

———

Over the course of time I did meet some soldiers who treated us like human beings. Once a guard came to me with toilet paper. He looked at me and said:

"I know that your God gives you strength."

"Are you a Muslim?" I asked.

"No," he said. "But I can see it. You've been living for so long in these small cages. No one can stand that. Sometimes we talk about it. You pray and God helps you. Otherwise you'd go crazy. If I had to live in this cage, I'd be sick within a few days."

That really surprised me.

There was also an older guard I had been observing for some time. Whenever anyone was being hit, he stood back and didn't take part. Even when he was assigned to an IRF team, he stayed outside the cage and refused to hit the prisoner. The other soldiers cursed him. But he just shook his head.

I spoke to him that day.

"I would like to ask you something."

"Go ahead . . ."

"Why didn't you take part just then?"

"I'm a human being just like you. What is happening here, is inhuman," he said.

That struck me.

The guard told me that he had a friend who had been in Vietnam and ended up in captivity there. After he was released, he had told him about his imprisonment and torture.

"I know what my friend went through. That must not happen again. It is incomprehensible that our government is doing the same to you as the Vietnamese did to the American prisoners. It's terrible!"

I occasionally ran into him in other cellblocks, but I never got the chance to speak to him again.

There was another guard who was in his mid-thirties. Whenever he was distributing food, he always asked me if I wanted another plateful. I also spoke to him a few times. He quite openly said that he didn't agree with what was happening in Guantanamo but that he signed up a long time ago. If he had known what it would be like at the time, he would have never joined the army, he said.

"When I arrived here," he said, "our superiors said you were killers and dangerous terrorists. They showed us movies about September 11 and gave us several weeks of training. Over and over again, they drove home how dangerous you were. I believed them at first. But then I saw you praying and reading the Koran. I found out that many of you are very friendly. I can even trust you. You don't take drugs, you don't steal and you don't commit adultery. I didn't know any of that before. You share your food even though you are all very hungry."

"MP" was written on the badge on his arm. All of the guards wore this badge, but this guard was different. He said that President Bush had ruined America's reputation in the world.

"Now I know the truth," he said. "I have seen it with my own eyes. I only have a few days left to serve. Then I'm finished with the Army."

He was working in my block on his last day. He came to me and said:

"Murat, I've only got two hours to go." He was very excited.

Then he came back and said: "Only one hour to go."

When his time was almost up, he reappeared, parked himself in front of the door of my cage and looked at his watch. There were a few guards standing a bit off to the side. He called them over.

"Hey, come and watch what I'm doing!"

The guards came closer. He looked at his watch and started to count.

"Five, four, three, two . . ."

When he counted to zero, he took off his armband. To the outrage of the other guards, he motioned as if he was about to wipe his butt with it. Then he threw the armband on the floor and stamped on it.

"I'm not an MP any more!"

He trampled on it in the way the guards had trampled on the Koran.

"You see that? That's it!"

I don't know whether he was punished for his actions. That evening he came back to my cage. I was sitting on the floor and he squatted down in front of my door.

"I'm sorry. I really hoped you would get out. I wanted to say goodbye." He had tears in his eyes.

"I'll try to help you when I get back to the States."

He pushed his fingers through the wire mesh. We said goodbye. I thanked him for his friendship and the many extra helpings that he gave me.

Unfortunately, I never asked him his name.

In September 2004, a guard brought a letter for me into my cage. It said that I was going to be brought in front of a military tribunal in Guantanamo. I was going to court? After all this time and all those interrogations? The tribunal was called the Combatant Status Review Tribunal. The tribunal would determine whether I was an enemy combatant. But I had never fought! Maybe the court would come to this very conclusion—and acquit me. The letter contained the words: "*George W. Bush, President of the United States of America v. Murat Kurnaz, plaintiff*."

They came to get me two weeks later. The hearing took place in an interrogation room. Was this another trick? No. There were no interrogators there, just three high-ranking officers sitting at a long table. I saw their epaulettes and their ribbons. A man sitting at a table at a right angle to the judges with a tape recorder in front of him read out that two colonels and a lieutenant were present. Sitting opposite him at another table was a man who could speak Turkish.

He said one of the three military personnel was my attorney. The others were the judge and the prosecutor.

The man in the middle, the judge, read something aloud, but I couldn't understand half of it. When the translator repeated it, I noticed two mistakes. For one thing, the judge said that police in Pakistan had questioned me about Selcuk. That was wrong. For another, it was stated that I had been taken to the military camp at Bagram from Pakistan even though I had been in Kandahar. How could a court make a mistake like that?

The translator said that I would be allowed to ask questions later.

He asked me whether I understood what the court was saying.

"Yes."

The judge continued to read aloud and then he said something that I could understand even in English:

"The prisoner had links with a person who was later involved in a suicide bomb attack. Selcuk Bilgin is the suicide bomber."

"Suicide? Bombings?"

"You can respond in a minute," the translator said.

"Would you like to make a statement?" the judge asked.

I was shocked. Selcuk? A suicide bomber? I asked the court when and where it allegedly happened. They weren't allowed to tell me that, the judge answered.

My whole world suddenly didn't make any sense. But these people didn't lie. It was a court after all. Was Selcuk dead? And had he killed a lot of people?

"I am here because Selcuk blew himself up?" I asked. "I didn't know. I didn't know that he was a terrorist. We worked out together and prayed in the mosque. We both had dogs. That's why we were friends. He was like a big brother to me. I didn't know he would do something like that. If he changed, I didn't notice. He never talked to me about anything like that. I don't need friends like that! My religion is peaceful."

The judge carried on.

Then they asked me what I was doing in Pakistan.

I explained.

After I had waited in vain for Selcuk at Karachi airport, I bought myself a telephone card, but the card didn't work. Someone had swindled me. But the second card worked. I called Selcuk's wife, but she hung up. Twice.

Then I flew to Islamabad to meet a guy named Hassan I had met on the plane. But I couldn't find him because he had given me a false address. So I traveled alone to Lahore to the Mansura Center. I was told the head of the center wasn't there, but that I should spend the night there and talk to him the next morning. In the morning I was given breakfast, but the center's director still had not arrived. Then in the office I was told that they wouldn't enroll me. I was a foreigner. It was too dangerous. I should go home. What was I supposed to do?

That morning—it was October 7, 2001—war had broken out in Afghanistan.

I was disappointed. I didn't want to go back home immediately and was determined to stay. The *tablighis* in Bremen had told me that *tablighis* in Pakistan traveled in small groups from mosque to mosque, studying there. So I would just join them. In any case, I didn't want to give up.

I caught a bus to Islamabad, where I went to a mosque and met a group of *tablighis*. At first they didn't trust me because I came from Germany. Maybe they thought I was a journalist. Then I got to know Mohammed. He was curious and spoke English well and he even knew a little Turkish. We joined the *tablighis* and slept in various mosques. New *tablighis* kept on joining us, while others would leave. Sometimes there were ten of us, sometimes thirty. The teaching lasted almost all day. In between, I walked through the city and explored the markets, the Kung Fu schools, and the snake charmers.

The court asked me if the *tablighis* gave me food, and I said yes. Every evening a few people would set off to the market to buy food for everyone. It was incredibly cheap. And every evening we argued about who would be allowed to go to the market. That was tradition, Mohammed said.

The judge wanted to know when and where I was arrested and what the Pakistani police had asked me.

I was amazed. Didn't they know?

_____

Two weeks after the hearing I was taken by an escort team and brought before the tribunal again. The judge read out the ruling. I was an enemy combatant, categorized as dangerous.

The judge justified the ruling by saying that I was a member of the Al Qaeda organization. The evidence that he cited was that I was a close friend of a suicide bomber and that I belonged to the Jama'at al-Tablighi because I had received support and food from this group.

"I would like to know whether I have to stay here or whether I can go home . . . ," I said.

"Mr. Attorney, do you have any questions on the prisoner's behalf?"

"No."

He had hardly said a single word throughout.

IX

GUANTANAMO
BAY, CAMP
ECHO

IN OCTOBER 2004, I WAS TRANSFERRED FROM CAMP 1 TO CAMP
Echo—I had been told it consisted entirely of solitary-confinement cells.

For all I knew, when the guards came and blindfolded me, they could
have been about to fly me back to Germany or Turkey. I believe I was
transported in a small, completely sealed bus. It felt as though I was in an
air-raid shelter on wheels. Everything I touched was made of metal. I
remember hoping that I wasn't being taken to Turkey.

After a ten-minute drive, the bus stopped and we got out. I couldn't
hear any sounds coming from other prisoners, just the noise of a wooden
door opening, then several metal ones. When they took off the blindfold,
I saw I was in a cage just like the ones in Camps 1 and 2, only smaller and
more solidly built, with a single toilet-sink unit like the ones found on
ships. A camera was mounted behind Plexiglas on the ceiling. The walls
were made of several layers of small chain-link fence, welded together so
that not even a spider would be able to slip through and visit me. I could
hardly see anything of the outside world. Directly in front of the cage
were a table and a chair. An iron ring was in the floor. I saw a wall with an

open door and then, a little way off, a second cage with a table and chair. I was totally isolated.

Later I found out that the Camp Echo contained a dozen small wooden houses with two cages each. I had no idea why I was there. Was this a new form of punishment? I had heard that several prisoners had disappeared after being taken to Camp Echo and no one knew whether they were still alive. The camp was designed so that the prisoners would never have to leave their own private cell-block. They could be interrogated directly in front of their cages, and each cell had its own tiny shower. Was this where I was going to have to spend the next few years?

The guards came three times a day to bring me my food—otherwise they were nowhere to be seen. Sometimes they skipped a meal. At night they no longer woke me up so frequently.

"Get up!"

"Why?"

"You've got a visit."

"A visit? Who would want to visit me?"

My curiosity was piqued. Surely, I thought, it was an interrogator who had been sent specially from Washington to "help" me. I couldn't wait to see what trick they'd try this time.

A portly man in his mid-thirties wearing a suit and glasses walked through the door. The guards shackled me to the iron ring and left us sitting alone at the table in front of my cage. The man was sweating profusely. His shirt was already soaked, and he fished a handkerchief from his pocket and wiped beads of the sweat from his brow.

"Hello."

The man removed his glasses and fiddled with them. He seemed nervous.

"I'm your attorney," he said in English.

"My attorney?" I had to laugh. "Is that a joke? You? An attorney?"

"I have a letter from your mother . . ."

They must have lost their minds, I thought. But I wanted to find out what they were up to.

"Let me see . . ."

It was indeed a letter from my mother. I recognized her handwriting immediately.

My dear son, it's me, your mother. I hope you're doing well. This man is Baher Azmy. You can trust him. He's your lawyer.

I couldn't believe my eyes. My first letter in three years! The first words I had had from my mother! She obviously hadn't been allowed to write any more than those few lines—otherwise the letter wouldn't have passed the military censors.

"Where did you get this?"

"I met your mother," the man said.

"Where?"

He told me that I had had a German attorney for years. He was my lawyer in the United States and would go to Germany to meet my family. He told me my mother had been to Turkey and Washington to help with my case.

In Washington?

That made me suspicious. Perhaps this man was an interrogator after all and was just using my mother's letter to gain my trust.

"How do I know that you're the lawyer in the letter?"

He removed a number of ID cards and documents from his pockets and briefcase and showed them to me. The name was the same on all of them.

"I am here to help you," he said.

"That's what they all say."

"Unfortunately the rules here are extremely strict. I have to write down everything you tell me and show it to them. And I can't come whenever I want. It's very difficult."

"Okay," I said. "Maybe you're a lawyer, maybe you're not. Documents can be faked. But I've got nothing to hide. I'll tell you whatever you want."

"I understand your skepticism," the man said.

The man who claimed to be my attorney showed me a brochure from a Turkish human-rights organization. In it were pictures of me, including a passport photo taken when I was seventeen or eighteen and still had short hair and no beard. There was also a picture of my mother in front of a big white building. The caption read: "Rabiye Kurnaz speaks to the American media in front of the Supreme Court Building in Washington." Another picture showed her crying. Underneath it were the words: "Any of us could be in the hell of Guantanamo."

The brochure filled me with sadness, but my curiosity was stronger.

I read how people were getting involved in my case. I studied the words on the brochure until I had learned them by heart. It said that the Turkish government had violated its own laws by refusing to get me out of here. I thought back about the two Turkish agents who had visited me and the charade they had put on. Further down in the brochure, it said that I was innocent. I could hardly believe it. There were people who thought I was innocent.

I realized that my mother had done everything in her power to save me. Even if she hadn't had any success yet, she knew where I was and that I was alive. That was the most important thing. I was gradually coming to believe that the man sitting across the table from me really was an attorney. They couldn't possibly have faked these pictures. But I was still going to have to watch what I said. He'd warned me, and the Americans were possibly listening in on our conversation. So I didn't tell him about being tortured. There was nothing he could do about *that* anyway.

"I only expect help from Allah," I told him. "But if Allah is willing, you will be the *sebeb*."

"The what?"

"The reason, the cause. The herald of my release."

Baher Azmy nodded, looking relieved.

"I have a suggestion," I said. "If you want to help me you can start right now."

"How?"

"The next time, bring some coffee. I haven't had any coffee in years. If you can do that, then we'll see. If you can't, you won't be able to get me freed anyway."

"I don't know if I can get you any coffee, but I'll try . . ."

"With lots of sugar," I said.

This was my first private visit since I had been taken prisoner.

I grabbed the letter from my mother and balled it up in my hand. Back in my cage I hid it under my clothes so that it would be hidden from the camera. But they took it away from me that night when they searched my cell.

That night, my head was full of thoughts. Could I really trust this man? Could a brochure like that be faked? Had the pictures of my mother been manipulated? But I didn't have anything to hide. They should have come to see that after all these years.

The next morning my attorney brought me a paper cup of coffee and a hot apple tart. The packaging said McDonald's. I was amazed. Did the guards have their own McDonald's outside the camp? The lawyer fished several sugar packets out of his pants pocket. This guy has already earned his keep, I thought.

During later visits, he brought some newspaper clippings for me from the *New York Times*, the *Washington Post*, and the German news magazines *Spiegel* and *Stern*. They were all writing about my case. He also mentioned that there were floods in Asia and that Germany had a new currency, the euro.

I read every article greedily. Some of the news was already old, but for me everything was new. In Guantanamo we didn't get any information from the outside world. Suddenly I came across an article that mentioned me. There was my picture, the same one from the Turkish brochure, with the caption: "The Taliban from Bremen." The Taliban from Bremen? That made my blood boil. Did people in Germany really think I was a Taliban? I had told the German agents my whole story when they interrogated me. Had they not confirmed it and reported it? Azmy shrugged. He said he was surprised to hear that people from the German government had visited me. I decided not to get angry about what people wrote about me. I wanted to be free any more. That was the only thing that mattered.

"Where's the part about Selcuk?" I asked.

"Selcuk?"

"My friend from Bremen who wanted to come to Pakistan with me. Where's the part about him blowing himself up. I can't find that . . ."

"Selcuk Bilgin blew himself up? Where did you get that idea?"

"He was a suicide bomber. I don't know where or why. The Americans told me during my hearing."

Again, Baher seemed amazed. He said there was no way Selcuk could be a suicide bomber. If a German or a Turkish resident of Germany had blown himself up, he would have known about it. The German and American press would have surely reported it.

I felt shattered. Why had the court claimed something like that?

Baher said that they might have confused Selcuk with someone else. It had to be a mistake.

"And Selcuk is the reason you're here?" he asked.

"Yes," I said. "And because I took food from the *tablighis*."

Baher shook his head and took some notes. For a while, neither of us spoke.

"Where is the prison courtyard?" he asked.

"Outside, in the cage."

"I didn't see it."

"What did you see?"

"Two camps. Metal containers. And then there was a small cage with a prisoner, in the middle of the camp."

"*That* is the prison courtyard," I said.

Baher got up, went to my cell and discreetly started examining it.

"This is how you've been living?"

I nodded.

"For all these years? I can't believe people would do this to their fellow human beings. How can you stand it? What did you do the whole time?"

"I waited."

Every day, for several days in a row, Baher Azmy visited me. Every time he came he brought newspaper clippings, which I read eagerly. One day he failed to arrive, and when he showed up the following day he was wearing different shoes. The guards had told him they couldn't let him in with his sandals because I might stomp on his feet and injure him. So he bought new shoes, sneakers. We had a good laugh about that. We got along well. Baher was born in Egypt and grew up in the United States. Only thirty-five years old, he was already teaching in law school. I told him everything he wanted to know, and he jotted down almost every word. Baher said he would write to me. He was going back and would try to get me released. He couldn't promise anything, but by now I trusted him. He asked if he could relay a message to my family on my behalf. I dictated a few sentences for my mother, to the effect that I was doing fine. Then I signed a document, giving him power of attorney. Then he said goodbye and left.

Later I discovered that I was one of the first three Guantanamo prisoners who were allowed to be visited by an attorney. The other two prisoners were from England. I saw Azmy three more times in the camp. After my release, he told me that he actually tried to visit me four times but on one occasion he had been told by the guards that I had refused to see him.

Several days after Azmy had left, I was taken back to Camp 2.

"Hey, Murat, where have you been?" asked Salah.

"I had a visitor, my lawyer in America."

Several prisoners laughed.

"Nonsense," said Salah. "They're pulling wool over your eyes."

"He brought me some newspaper clippings," I said.

That got everyone's attention and I promised to tell them what had been going on in the world after our evening prayers.

When the generators were briefly shut off that night, important news was passed from camp to camp. The last prisoner in a block would yell as loudly as possible in the direction of the next man. If the last prisoner in Block Alpha shouted, the first one in Block Bravo could hear what he was saying. The news was then relayed within the block, and the next night it would be yelled over to the next block. It was a time-consuming process since the guards and the IRF team came immediately to punish the prisoner who had done the yelling. But news did get through.

One thing was clear. When I was finished telling my news, others would have to take over the job. I knew that in a few minutes I would be heading for solitary confinement.

I split the news into two categories: world news and news that directly concerned the camp. I had a lot to tell. There had been a war in Iraq, and the Americans had won, but people were dying every day there in a civil war. There was a new government in Afghanistan. Concerning Guantanamo, a U.S. judge had declared the military tribunals unconstitutional, and George Bush had responded by saying that we detainees were all dangerous murderers and could not be compared to other prisoners. I recalled an absurd image from one of Baher's newspaper clippings. It was a picture of an American politician posing with a meal: half a chicken, potatoes, salad, soup, a soft drink, and some ice cream. He looked very satisfied. In the accompanying article, he claimed that that was what we were being given to eat in Guantanamo every day. The caption read: "Is chicken torture?"

I could only shake my head. In all those years, I didn't see anything like chicken, even in my dreams. Goddamn lies! Some newspaper reports said we were being treated with the same respect for human rights as the prisoners in ordinary American jails. But other articles had reported that some people in America were taking up our cause and beginning to speculate about torture in Guantanamo.

To ensure that all my news would get passed on, I spoke English as fast as I could. Salah translated it into Arabic. It wasn't long before the guards were spraying me with tear gas. I covered my face with my hands, crawled into the corner of my cell and kept talking.

I was taken to Block India, where they turned off the air conditioner. It was the harshest punishment there was. I immediately lay on the floor to minimize the amount of air I needed. I knew that for the next month I would hardly be able to breathe. I can't remember much from that time, but from one interrogation, when at least I got some air, I do recall the following exchange.

"Do you know where you made your mistake?" the interrogator asked me.

"You tell me."

"You talked to the others about Jihad and tried to get them stirred up. We didn't know you were such a good speaker. About Jihad."

Utter nonsense.

"You know exactly what I was talking about," I said. "The blocks are all bugged."

"I heard you had a visit from your attorney."

"That's none of your business."

"You should be on your guard. Are you sure he's an attorney? I hope you didn't sign anything."

"I did."

"That's your decision. Do you know what you signed?"

"What?"

"You'll see."

Six weeks later I was taken back to Camp 2. The news I had given Salah had been relayed through all the blocks—along with more information from the two prisoners from England who had been granted attorneys. We were connected with the world again! We knew what was happening outside Guantanamo! I have no idea how many prisoners had to pay for this achievement with time in the cooler.

X

GUANTANAMO BAY, CAMP 4

IT WAS A REAL PRIVILEGE. I DIDN'T KNOW WHAT I HAD DONE to deserve a transfer to Camp 4, but I had long since stopped asking about the whys and wherefores of Guantanamo. In Camp 4, or so we had heard, there were no cages. The prisoners lived together, and the food rations were bigger. The guards used to say you had to be on your best behavior to get to Camp 4. It was considered the best camp in Guantanamo.

Many prisoners, whole groups of them, had been released in the meantime—the Pakistanis, for example, and some of the Afghans. Almost all of them had been transferred to Camp 4 before they were set free. But there was no standard procedure. Sometimes in Camps 1 and 2, I had seen guards bringing civilian clothing—jeans, sneakers, and a T-shirt and denim jacket—to prisoners in their cages. A short time later, those prisoners were always gone. There was, we discovered, a way out of here after all. Baher Azmy had confirmed that the prisoners had been released and were living in their home countries.

Many of them were put straight back into prison by their own governments. The Americans had made this a condition for their release, our lawyers told us. In early 2006, a group of Saudis was allowed to go, but the Red Cross had warned them while they were still in Guantanamo that they were going straight to jail in Saudi Arabia. Our lawyers informed us about who had really been freed and who hadn't. Maybe some day, I thought, I would be sent to a German or Turkish prison.

Camp 4 was a dump. The cells were empty metal ship containers with only a metal slot in the door for sunlight and air. Space was cramped since each cell housed up to ten prisoners. The air was stale, and the ceiling light stayed on through the night. The generators hummed constantly just like Camps 1 and 2. It was like being in a ten-man oven.

During the day, the concrete floor got so hot you had to wear flip-flops to avoid burning the soles of your feet. I couldn't believe this was the best camp in Guantanamo. If there had been an air-conditioning unit, you could have made yourself somewhat comfortable there, but comfort wasn't the point. Without some sort of cooling system, we could have died in there so they installed a large rotating ceiling fan. But during the day, when the space was hottest, they turned the thing off. At night, when things began to cool down, they switched it back on—to make it more difficult for us to go to sleep. They only turned on the fan during the day when a helicopter arrived with a camera team. Camp 4 was the one journalists and photographers were allowed to visit.

We were allowed out more often for exercise. The prison "courtyard" was a corridor three feet wide by sixty feet long, running between the barbed-wire-protected containers. Several times a day, two cells—twenty prisoners in total—were allowed out for an hour. We spent the rest of the time in our cells under the never-blinking eyes of the surveillance cameras.

Once a week we were searched. We were herded into the cell and several IRF teams, perhaps two dozen soldiers in all, would arrive with machine guns and take up position outside the fencing. Two by two, we would be led to the washroom, where they frisked us. The other prisoners were kept confined within one of Camp 4's five containers while this was going on.

We were also inspected twice a week by groups of journalists. They never visited our containers, of course. Instead, we were led to a kind of playground with soccer goals, basketball hoops, and a volleyball net. Sometimes there were brand-new soccer balls, volleyballs, and basketballs lying around. Normally we weren't allowed on the grounds, only when journalists were visiting. As soon as the reporters left, the guards collected the balls. "Hurricane warning," they'd say, and take us back to the containers.

One time, I got up close enough to a group of journalists to make out what their guide was telling them. "Every block and every prisoner," he said, "is allowed two hours of soccer, volleyball or basketball per day."

———————

We did get more to eat in Camp 4 than in either Camp 1 or 2. We even got a glass of milk every morning. Because I was taking in more calories, I was able to work out more often. It was the same kind of food as before— a couple of bitter-tasting potatoes, cold vegetables, undercooked rice— but there was more of it. And we were allowed to share it amongst ourselves, which happened all the time because prisoners were constantly coming down with stomach ailments and couldn't eat.

Often, when we were let out for exercise, there was a cat at the fence. I called it 007 because it was so clever. As soon as it saw one of the guards, it ran away. It could tell the difference between the prisoners' clothing and the soldiers' uniforms. I used to save half of my milk for the cat.

I already knew several people in Camp 4. Abid, the Algerian from Germany, was there, as well as Musa, one of five Bosnians in Guantanamo. I had met Musa in Camp 1, and he had been my neighbor in solitary confinement during my one-man hunger strike.

Musa told me how the Bosnians had wound up in Guantanamo. Three of them were Arabs who had lived for years in Bosnia-Herzegovina, and they had all been arrested after September 11. The investigations had dragged on, before the case went to trial. At the hearing, the judge said that there was no evidence against them and that they were free to go. But when they tried to leave, a policeman told them to use the back door, where a masked commando of Americans was waiting for them. They were dragged into a car, taken to the airport, and flown to Cuba. Their families were waiting for them in front of the courthouse.

Secretly, I would work out with Musa and arm-wrestle with the Afghans in Camp 4. I usually won, but they were really good. They had all grown up in the mountains so they were used to carrying things around on their backs, and hiking up and down hills had made them very strong. In the washroom, I would practice karate moves or do sit-ups with Musa sitting on my shoulders. In the beginning, two cameras scanned the room, but we'd broken one of them and we could work out in a corner of the room out of view of the other. Once I lost my balance while doing a karate kick and slid into view.

I was sent to Romeo for a month. It was very hot because by then all the cell walls had been replaced with Plexiglas.

When I was caught working out a second time, I was sent to Romeo again and then transferred, as further punishment, back to Camp 1. I actually felt lucky about this after learning that there had been another incident involving the Koran in Camp 4. Some of the prisoners said a Koran had been torn up and thrown to the ground during a weekly search. There'd been a fight between the prisoners and the IRF teams in the container, and the prisoners in the other containers had heard what was going on.

Several hundred soldiers stormed the camp, firing rubber bullets from M-16s at the prisoners. Anyone outside the container got seriously injured. Once everyone outside had been shackled up, the soldiers opened a container containing a group of Afghan prisoners. The IRF teams sprayed tear gas and the soldiers fired rubber bullets, waiting for a moment before storming in.

That was a mistake.

The Afghans had torn the fan from the ceiling and had sharpened the rotor blades, using one blade to hone the next. The blades were like swords, and many of the soldiers suffered serious gashes. Prisoners had also tried to strangle their captors with cables from the ceiling-fan unit. The prisoners in Camp 1 said the Afghans had fought until they could no longer stand from exhaustion. None of the soldiers were killed, but one prisoner said he saw a lot of blood on the floor.

Camp 4 was completely evacuated, and a short time later there *were* casualties.

I was sleeping in my block in Camp 1 when, suddenly, a large group of soldiers came and woke us up, telling us to hand over our blankets, mattresses, and all our clothes. We knew something big had happened.

This next night news came from Bravo. Three people died, a prisoner yelled.

The following night we got their names. One of them was Yasser Talal al Zahrani from Saudi Arabia.

In late 2003, I had been in the same block as Yasser. He was the same age as me, a good-looking, friendly guy. Yasser had a nice voice and knew the Koran by heart so for a while he led our prayers. He was always optimistic, constantly repeating that we would be released in the near future. Sometimes, when he knew I was nearby, he would send his greetings.

He usually wanted to know if I was still secretly working out or whether I had given up.

Tell him I'm never giving up, I would answer.

I was very sad to hear Yasser was dead. I didn't know the other two people; one was a Saudi and the other was from Yemen. The guards said all three of them had committed suicide. Hung themselves.

———————

Several weeks later I got some new neighbors, who had been in Block Alpha the night Yasser and the other two men died. They had spoken to Yasser that day. They said that dinner had come early that evening and that everyone in the block suddenly got tired and had fallen asleep—even though it was never quiet in the block at that hour, even when the guards left us in peace. There was always someone who couldn't fall asleep, who wanted to pray or who kept waking up throughout the night. The metal shutters in front of the windows had also been closed from the outside, Yasser's last neighbor told us, as if a storm were approaching.

He said he had been woken up in the middle of the night by a loud bang and had seen the IRF team enter Yasser's cage. He didn't think twice about this and went back to sleep. A short time later, everyone was woken up by the guards, who made them hand over their mattresses, sheets, and clothes. Medics were already carrying Yasser out of his cage on a stretcher. The prisoners saw a piece of sheet in Yasser's mouth, and other pieces of sheet binding his arms and legs. There was more sheet around his neck, like a noose.

The Americans said he had hung himself. But we didn't think that could be true. He would have had to attach the noose to the sharp metal lattices with his hands and feet tied and with no chair to stand on. That was nearly impossible. There had been suicide attempts after the other incidents involving the Koran, but none of them had been successful, and the attempts were discovered immediately. Once I talked to Yasser about the idea of attempting suicide, but he had rejected it. He said our faith prohibited suicide.

It seemed highly unlikely that the guards would have failed to catch him in time. They barely let us out of their sight for a minute. Yasser would have needed several minutes to tie himself up like that and several more to actually die. It seemed suspicious when the Americans said that when they cut him down he had already been dead for a considerable time.

The guards claimed he had covered the walls of his cage so that he hadn't seen him do it. But what was he supposed to have used to cover the cage? The same sheets with which he had allegedly hung himself? And what about the rule prohibiting us from hanging anything on the walls of our cells?

It seemed too much of a coincidence that the other two dead men had hung themselves at exactly the same time in exactly the same way in the same block, while all the other inmates had been sleeping like babies.

When the guards were patrolling the corridors, it never took long before other guards came to ensure we were following the rules. The guards never took a break since they, too, were kept under surveillance to ensure they were carrying out their duties. Where had they been that night? And what about the sharpshooters in the watchtowers? Hadn't they noticed anything?

The other Saudi who had allegedly hung himself had been told a few days earlier that he was going to be released. Overjoyed, he had told everyone about it. In fact, a short time after the alleged suicides, a group of Saudis was sent home. This man didn't seem to have much of a reason for killing himself.

No, we prisoners unanimously agreed, the men had been killed. Maybe they had been beaten to death and then strung up, or perhaps they had been strangled. The question was: Why?

I had a theory. It could have been that the soldiers in Guantanamo were afraid of being sent to Iraq. Some of them spoke openly about not wanting to go over there. Maybe some of the guards and other soldiers thought that if prisoners died in Guantanamo, it would create trouble for the Bush government, and they wouldn't have to take part in the war.

A lot of Guantanamo prisoners believed in this theory. The generals paid very close attention to make sure that no prisoners died. The soldiers were allowed to torment us, put us in the coolers, deprive us of air, and chop off our fingers—as long as they didn't kill us. That was the big difference between Kandahar and Guantanamo, as we'd learned during the first hunger strikes in Camp X-Ray. They didn't want us to die.

Perhaps, the deaths of prisoners were being used against President Bush. It seemed like a suspicious coincidence that several weeks before, three prisoners had been poisoned. One evening, out of the blue, the guards had brought us baklava. They told us that the unusual gift was to celebrate the imminent release of a number of prisoners. Almost everyone ate it, but I was suspicious. The next morning one of the prisoners couldn't get up.

I had seen him fall sleep right after dinner, and when we knelt down for our morning prayers, he was lying in his cage, not moving. We noticed that there was white froth around his mouth and saw the medics take him away. A short time later we heard that two others had also been removed from their cells in a similar state.

A few days later, rumors began to circulate that all three had been poisoned. When the prisoners returned to their cells, they tried to tell us they had attempted suicide by taking pills. We didn't believe them. What sort of pills would they have taken, and how would they have gotten them? No one had any pills, and we were searched, orally as well, three times a day in Camp 1. When prisoners got sick and received medicine from the Americans, they were always searched with special care. We were convinced that during the interrogations the Americans had forced the prisoners to tell lies.

But who had poisoned the men? The guards prepared our food, and they were the ones who had given us the baklava. In retrospect, we figured that they had tried to poison the three men for the same reasons that they had killed the other three prisoners a few weeks later. The poison didn't work so they made sure the job was done right the second time around. That was my theory anyway. Other prisoners had different ideas. But we all agreed that the suicide story was fake.

After the prisoners' deaths, Camp 1 was evacuated and completely sealed off. A short while later, Camp 4 was reopened. I was one of the first prisoners transferred back there. After the riots earlier that year, only two of the containers were in use; each one housed six or seven of us. In my container I met the old Afghan man and his son from Camp X-Ray again. The father's name was Haji Zad. He was ninety-six years old, and he had just been reunited with his son for the first time in four years. Our cells were searched daily, and our food rations were reduced. It was hard for me to look at the old man because I felt so sorry for him.

———————

On two occasions in 2005 and 2006, the so-called Administrative Review Board took another look at my case. I refused to take part in the hearings, and there was nothing they could do about it. If they had beaten me or used pepper spray, I wouldn't have able to talk anyway. The tribunal went ahead in my absence. On both occasions, the escort team took me to the courtroom to hear the verdict being read out.

"The defendant was captured in Tora Bora in Afghanistan where he was leading a group of Taliban guerillas. He is considered an enemy combatant and will be kept in Guantanamo."

There were no more appeals.

"For five years," I protested, "you've known that I was arrested in Pakistan. What's this about?"

"That's what we've concluded from the evidence," said the head of the tribunal.

All my protests were in vain.

Soon after the verdict, I was brought to an interrogation room and chained to the floor. But no one came to ask me any questions. Hours later, two soldiers appeared and placed a telephone on the table.

"You'll be getting a call," they told me.

That made me curious. I didn't know who the caller would be. An interrogator? My lawyer? Maybe the judge?

More hours passed. What was going on here? Suddenly the phone rang. But no one came to help me.

I couldn't pick up the receiver with my hands and feet shackled, but the telephone kept ringing. I threw myself to the floor and tried to drag the table toward me with my feet. Kicking one of the table legs, I managed to dislodge the receiver and knock it down to the floor. I squirmed to get my head as close as possible to the handset. I could just hear a voice on the other end of the line.

"Hello? Hello?"

"Yes . . ."

"It's me, Baher. You're going to be released!"

"I know. How are you doing?"

"Murat, are you listening? You're going to be released."

"I know," I said. "They're playing a nasty trick on you. How is your daughter doing?"

"No, it's true. You're really going to be set free."

"Fine, if you say so. Remember how they called you a year ago and said I was already on my way to Turkey? You and my whole family flew over there to meet me. What did they say this time? Did they tell you when I was flying out?"

"I'm not allowed to say . . . just hold on!"

We said good-bye. Baher hung up, and I lay there on the floor listening to the dial tone.

I'd witnessed this trick once before. Prisoners would be brought to a plane, and they'd get in, having been told they were being flown home. Then they would be taken back to their cages. It was a way of breaking them psychologically.

About a week after the phone call, the escort team called my number in Camp 4. I was out alone in the yard getting some exercise when they threw a package of clothes over the fence. It landed on the gravel.

"Put these things on!"

I opened the package and examined what was inside: jeans, sneakers, a white T-shirt, and a denim jacket. I put them on. Was I really going to be released?

I went back to the container and said goodbye to the Afghans. I said that, if Allah was willing, I was now going to be set free. I told them to say goodbye to everyone for me. Then I took my leave.

I wished the old man was being released instead of me.

I didn't know where I was being taken. It could be Germany, Turkey, or back to Camp 1. Most likely, I was heading for a German or Turkish jail.

It was difficult to say goodbye to the other prisoners. They were staying behind and would continue to be tortured.

Just before I was supposed to be released, an officer held a document and a pen under my nose.

"Sign this piece of paper," he said, "saying that you were detained in Guantanamo Bay because you are linked to Al Qaeda and the Taliban. Or you are never going home."

After five years of imprisonment I was supposed to admit being a member of al Qaeda and the Taliban. Otherwise I wouldn't be sent home. After all the years, the interrogations, the torments, and the deaths, I was supposed to sign something affirming my guilt and exonerating them. Was this another one of their tricks?

I didn't sign anything.

They shackled me, put on the goggles, the soundproof headphones, and the gas mask, and led me into a hermetically sealed bus. We drove on board a ship and then back onto land. The door opened, and they briefly removed the goggles and the mask to inspect my hair and my beard. It was dark. Airplane motors were already running. The soldiers formed a semicircle around me before leading me up the loading ramp into the belly of the plane and shackling me to a seat in the middle of the cargo hold. I counted fifteen guards on board. Then they put my goggles and mask back on.

I was the only prisoner on the plane.

XI

RAMSTEIN AIR BASE, GERMANY

THEY LED ME DOWN A RAMP, AND THEN THE AMERICANS finally took off the goggles, the soundproof headphones and the gas mask. I was blinded by a harsh light. A large black vehicle was sitting on the runway, but the glare didn't come from the headlights because they weren't on. I saw three men in dark suits. They looked German.

The glare came from a watchtower—even though it was still day time. One of the men pressed a note into my hand. They exchanged nervous glances.

"Mr. Kurnaz," they said, "we've come to pick you up. You can trust us. Here's a letter from your mother."

Squinting, I tried to read the note. It was my mother's handwriting.

My dear son, Murat, these men are German officials. They're going to bring you to us. Your father, Ali, Alper and I are waiting outside together with your German and American lawyers.

Love, Mother.

The letter was dated August 24, 2006.

I had no idea it was August.

We got into a car, it was a Japanese brand, and one of the officials took the seat beside me. We were on an American army base—I could see military aircraft and hangars. The man next to me took out a small device, flipped it open, and typed something into it. Then he closed it and used it to make a telephone call.

"What is that?" I asked.

"A cell phone that also works as a miniature computer with a word processor."

My wrists and ankles still ached from the cuffs on the plane, which had been far too tight.

The other man, who was sitting up front, was talking into a radio. It crackled with static.

"Suspicious vehicle ahead, change direction. Drive . . ."

The driver braked, swerving to take a different route. I looked at the man next to me.

"It's the media," he said. "We're trying to avoid the media. We sent another car on ahead to distract them, but we're playing it safe."

I first truly realized then that I was in Germany, and perhaps, I thought, I'm really free now. At least they hadn't put me in handcuffs. The thing I most wanted to do was go to sleep—as soon as possible. But I also wanted to see my family. I didn't know what to say to the officials, so I said nothing.

The radio kept crackling, and each time it did we changed course.

We drove into a city. I didn't recognize the license plates and was overwhelmed by the sight of so many people and such bright colors. I hadn't seen anything like it for a long time. Where are we going? I asked.

"We're taking you to the Red Cross."

The car pulled into a parking lot in front of a large building that looked like a hotel. My first steps back on German soil, I thought. The building was an old people's home—at least that's what it said on the sign. A porter opened the door.

"Welcome, Mr. Kurnaz," a woman said, smiling at me. "I'm from the Red Cross."

Those were the first pleasant words I had heard in five years.

In the foyer, I saw signs, a dining room, a ballroom, and a toilet. The porter, the woman from the Red Cross, and the German officials led me into an elevator.

When the elevator doors opened, my family was standing in front of me. The first one I saw was my mother. She had lost a lot of weight. My brother Ali and my uncle were also there, but I didn't see Alper. And where is my father, I asked myself.

My mother took me in her arms and refused to let me go. She was crying. I was happy, but I didn't feel quite right with my mother crying like that. Afterward, the others hugged me too.

There was a whole table full of food in the adjoining room, but strangely enough I wasn't hungry. I should at least try a bit of food, I thought. The nice lady from the Red Cross had probably arranged all of it especially for me. Everything was so pleasant, and my family took out their cell phones to show me pictures of my aunts, nieces, and nephews. We took some pictures of ourselves and admired them on the screen. Everything seemed so unreal.

Why didn't my uncle say anything? I wondered.

Quietly, I asked my mother where my father was.

Then I realized I hadn't recognized my own father. Before I was captured, he was a powerful man who weighed more than two hundred pounds. Now he was as thin and gray as his older brother. I had also mistaken Alper for Ali. At the time I was captured, Alper had been only five—now he was ten. Ali had meanwhile grown up into a strapping young adult of eighteen years. It was as if I no longer knew him.

Alper sat on my lap. Everyone else crowded around me: Baher, my German lawyer, Bernhard Docke, the women from the Red Cross, the officials, and the doctor. My mother needed medical attention more than I did. The doctor gave her some pills to calm her nerves.

The lawyers wanted to know about my trip to Germany, about whether I had been shackled on board the plane and whether I'd been given something to eat and drink. The police then conferred with my attorneys. My mother was still crying softly, so I put my arm around her and pressed her close to me. As I did so, I became aware of the plastic band around my wrist, the green armband with my photo, the number 061 and the name "KUNN, MURAT."

Using two fingers, I tore it off before my family's eyes. They had interrogated, tormented, and tortured me nearly every day for five years, but they never learned how to spell my name correctly. Once, when I pointed this out, they beat me and accused me of giving them false information. They had repeatedly asked me what my name was over the years, and I'd even spelled it out for them.

I threw the arm band on the ground.

Ali picked it up and pocketed it.

That evening we drove away in my father's Mercedes. It was more than 300 miles to Bremen. We traveled through the unfamiliar city where I'd landed, with Baher and my German attorney leading the way in another car. It was like traveling through time.

Five years may not seem like such a long time. But if you spend five years in caged isolation, without television, newspapers, and radio, and cages and people in uniform are all you ever see, then it's as though you've returned from the Stone Age.

My mother, Ali, and Alper were sitting in the back seat. I thought about my wife and my uncle Ekram, who was like a friend and a brother to me. My uncle had told me about being sent to prison after getting in a knife fight, and I had thought about him a lot in Guantanamo. He was the only one who could have understood what it was like there.

We drove up an on-ramp to get on the highway, and I asked my father about my grandmother.

She died, he said, adding, "And there's someone else you loved who's dead."

I knew immediately who he was talking about, but I asked anyway.

"Is it Uncle Ekram?"

"Yes."

My heart sank.

I couldn't even bring myself to ask how he had died, but I knew then that the life I had left behind in Germany was no longer going to be as I had imagined it all those years in Guantanamo. My uncle Ekram would have been in his mid-thirties.

We drove for a while and Alper fell asleep. It had gotten dark. No one spoke.

My father was smoking cigarettes.

"As soon as I can," I said, "I'm going to bring Fatima to Germany."

My father looked at me.

"She won't come."

I was flabbergasted. We hadn't seen each other in five years, and we were man and wife. Of course she'd come!

"No, she won't be coming."

"Why not? I'll call her. She must know I've been released."

"She divorced you."

I didn't ask any more questions. My father drove on.

May Allah grant us whatever is good for us, I kept saying to myself.

What could I do? Fatima had waited for years without any sign that I was even alive. She had a right to get divorced. She was still young and didn't know whether I was ever coming back. She was a good woman, my father said later. She waited three years and hadn't heard a single word from me. If she had known you would be released, my father said, she would have waited—even if it had been ten years.

Today I'm happy for Fatima. I hope she has remarried and has a good life. I wish her happiness. But I have no contact with her. I don't want to remind her of the past.

The car in front of us signaled, and we turned into a rest stop. I got out of my father's Mercedes.

"I have coffee in the trunk," my mother said. "Do you want some?"

I love coffee.

My mother poured me a cup, and I looked up at the stars. It was the first time I'd seen a starry sky in five years. The nighttime sky was more beautiful than ever, and I realized at that moment precisely what they had taken from me in Guantanamo.

It was dark, and I was looking at the stars, a free man.

I forgot to drink the coffee.

When we arrived in Bremen, dozens of vehicles were parked in our tiny street. There were floodlights, catering vans, and buses with satellite dishes on their roofs. Photographers and cameramen were crowded in front of our house. I couldn't look. I didn't want to speak to any of them or let them take my picture.

The lawyers stopped their car, and Baher got out. I saw the journalists immediately surround him. Flashbulbs blazed like lightning. Baher and Bernhard walked a short distance past our house, and the pack of reporters followed them. My mother and I got out. Quickly, she put a blanket over my head. The next thing I knew I was in our front hall.

Photos of Baher were published in a number of newspapers. Some of the captions read: "The Taliban from Bremen returns home with a short beard and glasses."

That was how Baher also got to be a Taliban. Well, at least he was born in Egypt.

XII

BREMEN, HEMELINGEN

WENT DOWN TO THE BASEMENT AND TURNED ON THE LIGHT. I wanted to see my room, which was exactly as I had left it. Nothing had changed. Even the note I'd written a couple of days before my departure reminding myself to buy batteries was still on my desk. My parents hadn't touched anything, and Ali and Alper hadn't been in there playing. It was a strange feeling—seeing my black leather couch, my blue sofa bed, my glass-fronted wardrobe, and my model ship again. I'd decorated my room when I was thirteen and had never changed a thing.

There was a case under my wardrobe. I pulled it out and removed the old slide projector my uncle Ekram had given me. I looked at it for a while and then went into the living room.

My family was sitting around our living-room table, everyone except Alper, who had gone to bed. The television set was on quietly in the background, and I stared at the screen for a while. Ali took out his wallet and showed me euro bills and coins. It looked like play money. The fan in the corner was running, and my mother and Ali complained that the room was too cold. But I found it pleasantly cool.

"Son, you must be hungry," my mother said.

The pots were on the stove. They had prepared Turkish mince-meat burgers, lamb, kebabs, rice, green beans, French fries, potatoes, and a couple of different soups. They must have been cooking for days. I opened the refrigerator. It was like being in paradise. I sat down on the tile floor in front of it and removed everything down to the last jar of mustard. I piled it all up in front of me and tried to decide what I would eat first and what second: spicy peppers-and-rice soup, cheese, meat patties, olives, kebabs, green beans, baklava, pickles . . .

I decided to have a Kit-Kat.

I ate a whole package of them.

I ate everything I could.

I didn't know how late it was, and I didn't care. I could always pull the curtains in my room. My father was already asleep, and my mother had made my sofa bed. It was the first time in five years that she had done anything in my room. I folded the bed back up, pushed the desk to one side and lay down on the carpet. It was dark. That was something completely new, I thought, going to sleep in the dark. I lay my head on the soft pillow and smelled the blanket. My mother had dried the laundry, as always, outside on the clothesline.

It was totally still.

Tonight no one would come to search or beat me.

For the first time in almost five years, I got a great night's sleep.

The next day Bernhard came with Baher, who wanted to say goodbye.

That was just the beginning of the excitement. My father had disconnected the doorbell and the telephone to keep us from being besieged by reporters, but I took the phone into my room, reconnected it, and called just about everyone I know. It was great fun calling people again. My door was constantly opening to let in relatives who wanted to see me.

Everyone brought me something to eat, and of course I tasted it all. Then my friends came. Some of them stayed deep into the night, and the next day it was more of the same. It took several weeks before I had seen everyone again. In my free moments, I said my prayers.

I didn't talk to my parents about what had happened to me in Guantanamo. I spent a lot of time listening to my relatives and friends. They didn't ask me any questions, although I would have answered them, if they had.

No one wanted to know about Guantanamo, except Bernhard—he was constantly asking me questions.

The photographers and cameramen continued waiting outside our house for around ten days. Then most of them left. I waited for three weeks before daring to sneak out of the house. Two friends from Hemelingen visited me, and we borrowed my father's Mercedes. After all those years, I finally got to drive a car again, and we went to the spot by the river with the wharf and the junkyard where I had played and gone fishing as a child. It was dark by the time we got there. We walked for a while in the yellow glow of the warehouse lights, and I sat on a bollard and stared at the water.

Only then did I feel that I was truly back at home.

I still enjoy walking alone by the river. I used to go there on my bicycle— now I take my motorbike. It's great driving a motorbike along the new streets. There's an industrial park now along the banks of the Weser River where there once used to be fields of potato and corn. But the lake still smells like coffee. I come here a lot in the evening to regain my peace of mind.

Since I've returned to Bremen, I seldom walk anywhere. I prefer taking my father's car or my motorbike. I wouldn't get far on foot. I tried it a few times, but I kept getting stopped by people who wanted to take pictures. Some even asked for my autograph. Most of them are friendly and ask me a couple of questions. But I can't answer all of them, and I don't want to seem arrogant if I say no.

I know that I stick out from the crowd with my long beard and hair. But I like my beard. I think it looks nice, and growing a beard was the only freedom I enjoyed in Guantanamo.

Recently a young man came up to me on the street in Hemelingen, the kid brother of one of my childhood friends. Now in his mid-twenties, he said he'd done three years in a Bremen jail, and while he was there, he collected everything that was written about me. It was almost as if I were a kind of a role model for him. People who have been in prison themselves always seem to be especially interested in my story.

One day the mayor of Bremen paid us a visit. He brought a bouquet of flowers and said he had nothing to do with the previous city government, who had tried to revoke my residency permit. He wanted to welcome me back. He was the only authority who did so. No one, other than my lawyer, ever asked me if I needed medical, psychological, or any other kind of help.

Until recently, I had no health insurance because they said I either had to have a job or be on welfare to qualify. I tried to apply for welfare benefits, but no one offered me any assistance. I was always missing this or that piece of paper. In the end, I gave up. Today I have a job—working for the city of Bremen on social projects.

One day there was a fire in our neighborhood. I had just come back from a motorcycle ride and was still wearing my helmet and a face mask underneath. I could smell smoke in the hallway of our house. I ran upstairs, and the smoke got stronger. I shut the windows and went out to see where it was coming from.

The auto-repair garage at the end of our street was on fire, and the pitch-black smoke from burning tires was blowing over to our house. The fire trucks had already arrived on the scene, and a lot of people from our neighborhood were watching them put out the blaze. I was still wearing my motorcycle jacket and kept my face mask on to protect myself from the smoke. When the police arrived, I asked one of the officers if it wouldn't be better to evacuate the surrounding houses.

"Everything's under control," the officer said.

I looked at the fire. Cameramen were showing up.

A little while later, a policeman approached me and asked to see my face. I took off the mask.

"Now I know who you are," the policeman said.

He went to his patrol car and said something into the radio. Then he returned.

"Why are you wearing a mask?"

"Because of the fire. I was riding my motorcycle and I left it on to protect myself from the smoke."

He asked to see my passport, but I only had my driver's license with me.

"Where's your motorcycle?"

"Right outside. Do you want to see it?"

"No. We're taking you in to investigate if you've been involved in an act of arson."

On the way to the station, my mother called me on my cell phone.

"Talk in German, not in Turkish," the policeman hissed.

I told my mother that I was being taken to the police station and explained why. I asked the officer whether they would take me back home or whether I should have my mother come pick me up. He didn't answer. At the station, the officers said I would have to get completely undressed, so they could see whether I had any flammable liquids on me. I told them my religion prohibited me from taking all my clothes off in front of them.

One of the officers said, "Then we'll get one of our colleagues and make you. You won't enjoy it!"

I suggested that they close the windows and I cover my private parts with my jacket.

They agreed.

I don't smoke. I didn't even have a lighter on me.

It's not a story I look back on happily. My mother got an unnecessary scare, and I had to ask myself why, out of more than hundred people on the street, I was the only one who had to go to the police station. Did the police still suspect me of being a terrorist? Or a Taliban fighter who sets tires on fire at a garage six hundred feet from his own home?

In late 2006, Bremen's criminal police department took a statement from me about the two German soldiers who had beaten me in Kandahar. I was supposed to identify them from photographs. I went with Bernhard to the police department, where they wanted to search us for weapons at the door. Bernhard protested. I was here as a witness, he said, not as a suspect.

Were they afraid of me?

For a long time I suspected I was being kept under surveillance. Sometimes I heard a strange echo on our phone. Sometimes a delivery van would be parked on the street in front of our house for what I thought was a suspiciously long time. Once a letter concerning this book didn't arrive at my house. But maybe these were all coincidences.

My statements to the media led the German parliament, the Bundestag, to set up two special investigative committees to look into whether the previous German government was complicit in my detention and whether German soldiers had mistreated me. I have since testified before that committee and well as one set up by the EU in Brussels to investigate possible illegal CIA operations in Europe. During a break in the proceedings, an official who had brought me to my family after I landed in Ramstein came up to me and said: "I never knew about all this."

What I didn't know was that the Americans had allegedly decided as early as 2002 that I was innocent and were willing to let me go. That shocked me. Why didn't they just release me, then?

I discovered that the German government apparently didn't want to let me reenter the country, and claimed that my residency permit had expired because I hadn't applied for an extension on time. Of course, I couldn't file for the extension because I was in Guantanamo, and even if I had thought of it, the Americans would have laughed at me and sent me to the cooler.

My lawyer told me that government officials had even tried to get the Americans to send them my passport so that they could void my residency permit. I don't know whether this is true. If it turns out that they allowed me to be tortured, when they could have prevented it, I'm speechless.

Today, I have a permanent residency permit and would like to become a German citizen. I don't know whether I will get citizenship, but I'd like to stay in Germany and live and work in Hemelingen. I was born, grew up, and went to school here like most people I know. We may speak Turkish at home, but I live in Germany and feel like a German. I'm especially grateful to Germany's current Chancellor Angela Merkel for getting personally involved to help secure my release.

The country of which I am a citizen, Turkey, did nothing for me, and now they want me to do military service. They wasted no time trying to get me in the army. The letter asking me to report arrived one day after I got back to Hemelingen from Guantanamo.

My friend Selcuk, who was mistaken for a suicide bomber, still lives in Bremen, and I've heard he's become a father. I don't know what he really believed or did back then. I never saw him again. I'm not angry that he never came to Karachi, but I don't want to have any contact with him. I want to start a new life and make new friends.

Things might have turned out differently if Selcuk's brother hadn't told the border police in Frankfurt that we intended to go to Afghanistan and fight with the Taliban. But you can't change the past. I read in a newspaper that Selcuk's brother has since retracted his statement.

With time, I have come to understand how I got caught up in the mill of a major international political conflict, although I still can't grasp how certain things fit together. What I do know is that ever since January 2007, which is when I testified in front of the special investigations committee of the Bundestag in Berlin, I have once again unwillingly become a political figure in Germany.

All I did was tell people what happened to me, and I was happy that someone listened. But since then, it seems as though I constantly have to defend myself against accusations of being a terrorist—even though both the Americans and Germans who interrogated me in Guantanamo, as well as the prosecutors in Bremen, all concluded that I was clearly innocent. I hope that some day no one will doubt my innocence any more. But there's something else that's even more important to me.

The moderator of a Turkish television news show once asked me whether I'd seen the movie *The Road to Guantanamo*. He wanted to know how realistic it was. I said that it was a good movie, but that it only depicted some of the truth.

It's important that our stories are told. We need to counter the endless reports written in Guantanamo itself. We have to speak up and say: I tried to hand back my blanket and got four weeks in solitary confinement. We have to tell the world how Abdul lost his legs and how the Moroccan captain lost his fingers. The world needs to know about the prisoners who died in Kandahar. We have to describe how the doctors came only to check whether we were dead or could stand to be tortured for a little longer.

Did Guantanamo change me? I don't think so. I believe I've remained the same person I always was, with the same name, living in the same house. At the end of the interview with the Turkish TV show, the moderator asked me what I wanted to do when this book was finished. I said I wanted to get married, if God was willing, and start a family.

On the other hand, maybe Guantanamo did change me. I now know what people are capable of doing to their fellow human beings, and how politicians speak and act. I have a new appreciation for the value of simple things like sleeping and eating. Of being free.

Maybe you can picture my situation like this. Right now I'm sitting in my room with everything I need: Internet access, television, a phone, and enough to eat. I have my weights, and I can do sports. But what would happen if someone locked the door and imprisoned me? How long would someone last in this room? Twenty-four hours wouldn't be a problem, and maybe a week wouldn't be too bad either. But months? Perhaps you can imagine then how difficult it is for the prisoners still being held in Guantanamo.

I think a lot about their suffering. While I sit here eating chocolate bars and peeling mandarin oranges, they are being beaten and starved. I think less about my own time there than about the people who were only fourteen years old when they were captured, and have spent their youth being tortured. I can eat, drink, and sleep much the same as I did five years ago, but I never forget that people are being abused in Cuba. It makes me sad when I think of them.

I pray that they will be released and that the camp will be shut down.

———————

I've never talked with my mother and father about Guantanamo, and they've never asked me about it. Maybe that's just a question of time.

———————

Once I was looking out the window at the snow falling. My mother came up to me and asked whether it had ever snowed in Cuba.

No, mother, I said. Of course not.

It never snows in Cuba.

EPILOGUE

Baher Azmy

NTIL THE SUMMER OF 2004, WHEN THE GUANTANAMO camps were opened up to law and lawyers and, therefore, to minimal scrutiny, Bush Administration officials repeatedly claimed that Guantanamo held only the "worst of the worst" or "the most dangerous, best trained, vicious killers on the face of the earth" or, in one particularly colorful phrasing, men who "would gnaw the hydraulic lines of a C-17 to bring it down." Along with other central assertions made in support of Guantanamo—that the "terrorist" detainees were not entitled to recognition of any legal rights whatsoever but that they were neverthe- less treated humanely by American personnel—this confident boast perhaps would assuage an otherwise reluctant public to accept the administration's deeply anomalous experiment in Guantanamo.

At the time of this writing, however, the administration's Guantanamo project is doomed to fail not just because of the accumu- lating weight of international pressure, but also largely because once Guantanamo's cloak of secrecy was pierced, the truth about detainees and the administration's often brutal treatment and incompetent decisions on whom to imprison has slowly emerged. As demonstrated by this powerful memoir, Murat's case lays to shameful waste the administration's defense of Guantanamo. Indeed, not only is Murat innocent of any connections with the Taliban, Al Qaeda, or any other terrorist groups, it is now clear that the U.S. government knew of his innocence as early as 2002 (just six months into his detention), even as it continued, cynically, to argue that Murat was an "enemy combatant." The Schroeder government in Germany also, it turns out, had collaborated with the Americans for years in preventing Murat's release to Germany, at the same time that German government officials were self-righteously criticizing the prison camp and protesting that there was nothing they could do to help free Murat. Like a malignant cancer, the corruption of Guantanamo spreads deep and wide. No one has yet assumed responsibility for this hypocrisy and for the egregiously unjust five-year term of abuse and imprisonment for Murat. A genuine remedy for Murat's suffering may never come, but the telling of his remarkable story might represent an important start.

I didn't know Murat was innocent when I agreed to represent him in the summer of 2004. At that early stage in our long struggle together, who Murat was, or what he did, seemed largely irrelevant. As a lawyer, professor of constitutional law, and concerned citizen, I had been deeply troubled with the Bush Administration's astonishing assertion of executive power—a power that would authorize the arrest of any person, anywhere in the world, for alleged acts of terrorism or association with terrorists, on nothing more than the president's say-so. And, in denying the applicability of any law—domestic, international or military—to Guantanamo, the president was asserting the power to do anything he or his commanders wanted at any time, in total darkness, regardless of the consequences. So, in agreeing to represent Murat, I hoped, like many other lawyers involved in defending Guantanamo detainees, to vindicate a principle: that there should be no prison beyond the law.

Following the Supreme Court's decision in 2004 that entitled the detainees to challenge the legality of their detentions, lawyers from the Center for Constitutional Rights and I filed a bare bones legal petition for a writ of habeas corpus in U.S. court in Washington, D.C., naming George Bush and others as defendants. This ancient legal device, one the United States inherited from old English common law, requires the executive to justify the legal and factual basis of the prisoner's detention before a neutral judge; and has long been considered the bulwark of liberty and the best check against arbitrary executive power and imprisonments. One remarkable aspect of our habeas filing—utterly unique in my experience as a lawyer—was that my client didn't authorize me to file it, nor did he even know a case or a lawyer existed. Because he couldn't file the petition on his own behalf, it was filed in his mother's name, Rabiye Kurnaz, who was called Murat's "Next Friend." This maneuver was the first of a number of procedures or arguments we would employ that seemed more to resemble ancient English practice—for example, when a king would imprison a political enemy in a remote tower—than routine American legal practice.

Soon thereafter, I completed the process to get a "secret" security clearance from the government, which they required before I could talk to my client or see the classified evidence against him. According to the government, every detainee in Guantanamo was an "enemy combatant"; therefore, everything out of a detainee's mouth—a statement about the weather, his health, how he was treated—was presumptively deemed classified information and could not therefore be disclosed without first being cleared by government officials. This was an incredibly burdensome process, and it was only one of many. We were not allowed to speak to the detainees on the phone, and our letters, also subject to inspection by the government, routinely took weeks to reach clients. One time I asked the government to investigate why I hadn't received a letter I had expected from Murat and learned that it was sitting in a bag with dozens of other detainee letters, accidentally sent to the Department of Homeland Security mailroom.

Also, Continental does not fly to Guantanamo. Getting there, even after receiving government clearance to visit, is exhausting and expensive. For my first visit in October 2004, I was accompanied by a German translator, Belinda, and we flew to Fort Lauderdale and then took a government-cleared charter propeller plane by a service called, absurdly, Air Sunshine, around forbidden Cuban airspace and into the Guantanamo airfield. Once on the base, we were driven around in a small school bus by an affable marine escort nicknamed "Gunny."

I was the third civilian lawyer to enter the Guantanamo prison camps. I won't ever forget the incredible anxiety I felt in the moments before my first meeting with Murat. Though I had thought hard about what I would say to him, in fact, no amount of preparation or experience could fully comfort me in this bizarre, intimidating place. As I walked through several fifteen-foot high locked gates and into Camp Echo's inner sanctum, across gravel made bright white by the blazing Caribbean sun, my status as a civilian and a lawyer—formal shoes and tie—was reinforced by the sounds of practice machine-gun fire in the distance. Inside, the Camp was impossibly spare, quiet, and hot. You could hear nothing from the self-contained cells holding the prisoners; they couldn't be seen from the courtyard either. The only perceptible noise came from overworked air conditioners and the crunch of military boots against the white gravel.

After a few minutes of waiting in this courtyard, the impossibly young military guard who had been preparing Murat for my visit came up to inform me that Murat claimed he didn't want the German translator I had flown down with me in our meeting.

"He speaks English?" I asked, incredulously.

"Yeah, it ain't so good, but you can basically understand him," the guard replied.

"What? Since when?" I insisted.

The guard didn't know, and obviously neither did Murat's family, who hadn't been allowed to communicate with him in the three years since his detention began.

Belinda went back to our dormitory-style barracks on the other side of the island until she could get a flight home, while I prepared myself to meet Murat alone. When the door to the tiny meeting room opened, Murat was seated, squinting at the incoming sunlight. Dressed in a short, tan shirt and cotton pants, with a flowing beard and red-brown mane of hair, he looked like someone who had been shipwrecked on a desert island, which, in a sense, he was. He shook my hand and motioned for me to sit across from him on the flimsy plastic chair, as if he were welcoming me to tea in his home. With my first words, I tried to sound confident.

"Murat, my name is Baher Azmy. I am a lawyer. I do not work for the U.S. government. Your family in Germany asked me to help you."

I handed him the handwritten note from his worried mother that I had cleared by the military at the last minute, to help convince him I was on his side. This was a considerable concern, since in three years he had not talked to anyone who was not military personnel or an interrogator, had no knowledge of any legal proceedings, and had no reason to trust anyone who approached him. As I watched his pained expression while reading the loving note from his mother—his first taste of humanity in three years—I felt as though I was delivering a crumb of bread to Robinson Crusoe.

I then explained that his mother and a German lawyer, Bernhard Docke, had been fighting for years for him back home, and that, following a recent Supreme Court decision, I had filed a case for him in U.S. court in an attempt to challenge his detention. I also told him I was born in Egypt, that I was a Muslim, and a law professor with great faith in the American legal system. He was unfailingly polite, disarmingly warm, but understandably skeptical, it seemed. After more discussion, he asked: "You have sued President Bush?"

"Yes," I answered, "you and I have sued him. And, I will do everything I can to help you."

He paused, stroked the ends of his beard resting at his hips and replied in a heavy German accent—to my considerable relief—"This is goot." We spent eight hours a day for the next four days talking—about everything—and on four subsequent visits I spent dozens of hours with him.

He told me about Selcuk, his trip to the Frankfurt Airport, the Tablighis, his arrest in Pakistan. On the second day, I pressed and pushed him on his story; who did you meet, where did you go, did you even have any interest in Afghanistan? Though it is not a lawyer's role to assure himself of a client's innocence, I was becoming quite convinced that his story, punctuated with precise details, held together very well. I didn't ask about his treatment by military personnel; that traumatic discussion would have to come in the future. He asked me about my family, told me about summers in Turkey and engaged in sarcastic and often dark humor that I had thought I could only find in certain cynical corridors in New York. Murat dealt with his horrible situation—the endless boredom, the brutal injustice, the aura of forever that hangs over the whole of Guantanamo—through a rooted and hopeful faith in Islam; this he would express to me in meaningful but not proselytizing manner. But, to be sure, his eye for noticing the absurd was also a good tonic.

As afternoons wore on, on this first trip and subsequent ones, we laughed hilariously about his depiction of the incompetence of the Pakistani police, the absurd redundancy of his interrogations (obsessed as they seemed to be with confirming his birth date or the correct spelling of his name) and the sad state of the Gitmo detainee menu. Once, after Murat wounded a fly hovering around our table with a coffee stirrer, we joked that this act of hostility was sure to get him designated as an enemy combatant. We toyed for a while with the image of him being forced to answer to another military tribunal or interrogator for either "associating with" such a known and sometimes mortal enemy of the United States, or for otherwise revealing an obvious propensity for violence and terrorism.

As Murat describes, I brought him McDonald's coffee and an apple pie—which he ate with wondrous nostalgia for his mother's version. On subsequent visits, I became more adventurous in what I would bring to our meetings: dolmas, baklava, cheese, pita bread, Turkish figs, fresh garlic (his request), subs, pizza, filet o'fish sandwiches, fries, hot peppers (also his request), Jolly Ranchers, cookies, fresh fruit, canned fruit, dried fruit, melting McFlurries, and even a packaged shrimp cocktail. I was shopping for a starving man. I also brought him Starbucks but, to my surprise, he preferred McDonald's coffee. It's an interesting bit of consumerist trivia, an absurdly dark one really, when one considers that just about a mile from the strip mall housing those and other fronts of innocent Americana, there existed a camp housing a fully constructed project of dehumanization.

On this first trip we did some legal work as well. We needed an affidavit for his German immigration case, demonstrating the otherwise self-evident proposition that while held in Guantanamo, he did not have much of an opportunity to renew his German residency status. A translator would certainly have been helpful, with tenses and declensions to negotiate, but we managed. This was an important document—his first statement to the outside world. But, like a lawyer for a client on a desert island, I had to handwrite the affidavit on ruled paper for his signature there—no computers or typewriters or easy revisions.

Our first good-bye was deeply affecting for me. We embraced for a long time with promises to write and visit together again. These were moments of intense optimism; perhaps by being there, I and other lawyers would be shining a small light in a dark and depressing place. By the time of my evening flight over the Caribbean, however, I was a wreck—physically exhausted and emotionally overwhelmed at the prospect of leaving Murat behind to endure for more months inside a cage fit for animals at best. This case, of course, became for me far more than an effort to vindicate an abstract principle. Murat was not a pawn in some epic constitutional struggle; he was a living, caring, and profoundly human being, who I was convinced should be comfortably at home in the company of his mother, brothers, and friends.

Soon after I returned to the United States, I met Bernhard, my German co-counsel, who was visiting New York with his son. We hit it off immediately, a happy development considering the hundreds of hours we spent together in Bremen, Berlin, Bavaria (to pick up Murat when he was released), and even Istanbul working on his case. Bernhard was with me when we received the government's answer to our habeas corpus petition—the supposed reasons for his detention, which came out of the Combatant Status Review Tribunal process Murat describes in this book. The charges were, as Murat notes here, preposterous.

First, there was no allegation that Murat entered Afghanistan, met any terrorists, or held a weapon. The government actually contended that Murat Kurnaz was an "enemy combatant" because his friend Selcuk Bilgin "engaged" in a suicide bombing and was possibly responsible for a suicide bombing in an Istanbul synagogue in November 2003. Leaving aside the astonishing legal proposition that one could spend the rest of one's life in prison because of the unknown acts of a friend (Murat had already been in Guantanamo for eighteen months by the time of this alleged suicide bombing), it was factually absurd. As a five-minute call to the appropriate German authorities would have revealed, Selcuk was alive and well in Bremen. Bernhard knew this and had the awkward duty of securing an affidavit from Selcuk stating that, "um, I am alive." My mischievous side still regrets not taking a picture next to Selcuk during our meeting in 2005, perhaps holding up a dated copy of a newspaper, and sending it to the government or filing it in court in order to rebut the suicide bomber charge.

The government also claimed that Murat was an enemy combatant, not because he undertook any hostile actions or even thoughts, but because he associated with the Tablighis, a group that apparently has some members who at some point in time have supported groups hostile to the United States. We obtained letters from three prominent experts on this group and submitted them to the U.S. government, demonstrating the consensus view that the Tablighis are an avowedly peaceful and apolitical group. But, things should never even have gotten that far; at the outset, the government's theory of guilt by association would justify the imprisonment of the several million followers of this group and others, because of what a few members might have at some time done. The government has actually admitted as much. In a hearing in federal court in late 2004, government lawyers conceded in response to a question from a skeptical judge that, under their conception, a "little old lady from Switzerland" who gives money to what she believes is an Afghan orphanage but which, unbeknownst to her, turns out to be a front for the Taliban could be detained in Guantanamo as an enemy combatant.* Legally, if obviously not physically, Murat was not very different from the little old lady from Switzerland.

Still, I thought perhaps the government might have some other troubling evidence in the classified portion of Murat's file, which I was permitted to review in government "secure facility" near Washington. When I did review it, I was stunned. There was nothing. Indeed, as has been reported, there are a number of statements from military intelligence that actually concluded that he had no connections to Al Qaeda, the Taliban, or any other terrorist threat. The government has continued to try to keep this embarrassing set of revelations secret, even after the *Washington Post* published them on its front page in March 2005. We recently sued the Department of Defense in federal court in an attempt to declassify all of the substantial exculpatory material in Murat's file.

In January 2005, three months after the government provided the records of the Combatant Status Review Tribunals upon which the government "enemy combatant" decisions were based, a federal Judge, Joyce Hens Green, ruled on the legality of the government's detention scheme. Judge Green held that, contrary to the government's position, the detainees were entitled to fundamental due process rights to challenge their detention, and that the CSRT hearing system instituted by the government—with its many grotesque procedural defects—fell far short of what was minimally constitutionally required. What was particularly remarkable about the decision is that Judge Green singled out Murat's case, among the sixty-five she reviewed, as one that "highlights" the inadequacy of the CSRT system. She concluded that the basis for the government's enemy combatant determination—mere associations either

---

* See In re Guantanamo Bay Detainee Cases, 355 F. Supp. 2d 443 (D.D. C. 2005).

with an alleged suicide bomber and a large missionary Islamic group—was insufficient, even if true, to justify his detention. She noted that Murat had no knowledge or hand in wrongdoing committed by either of these parties and that the evidence suggested that Murat was in Pakistan only to study the Koran.

Most important, Judge Green cited numerous statements in Murat's file that demonstrated that he was in fact innocent of any connections with terrorism but which were apparently ignored by the Tribunal, which determined Murat to be an "enemy combatant." In sum, Judge Green concluded Murat's detention was unlawful. The decision, which came out January 31, 2005, was a tremendous development in his case. However, while we were in the early stages of preparing a motion, based on this ruling, requesting the court to order his release, the government appealed Judge Green's decision and successfully obtained an order freezing the impact of her momentous ruling until it could be reviewed by the appellate court. (Judge Green's ruling, and the appellate court's decision to reverse it, will have been considered by the United States Supreme Court at the time of this book's publication).

The appeal of Judge Green's decision meant legal proceedings were at a standstill. We therefore resorted to other forms of advocacy to draw attention to Murat's case. I met with German consular officials in Washington and traveled to Germany to join Bernhard in publicizing Murat's plight. Bernhard and I reasoned that, because no detainees had yet been released as a result of any court ruling, we had to pressure—or more likely shame—the German government to negotiate for his release.

During this visit to Germany, in March 2005, I met Rabiye, Murat's mother, and Ali, Murat's fifteen-year-old brother, in Bernhard's office.* Rabiye was warm and gracious toward me, if a little hesitant to talk. Through Bernhard's translation, she thanked me for helping "my Murat"

---

* I had spoken to Murat's family by phone and received his mother's handwritten note I presented to him, by fax, before I met with Murat. I first met the Kurnaz family in March, after my second trip to visit Murat.

and thanked me again and again when I reported that he was in relatively good spirits and health, as if I had anything to do with the content of this message. Rabiye and Ali were especially delighted to hear my amazement over the resemblance between Ali—especially his smile, voice, and manner—and Murat. I suppose we all marvel when we notice human likenesses; but the scene was intensely discordant for me as I recognized in one brother before me, the essential characteristics of another I had only seen locked in a cage on the other side of the world.

The next day, in front of a packed press corps, I disclosed Murat's allegations of the torture he suffered in Kandahar and Guantanamo as well as the evidence of his innocence, all of it new to the German media. As I listed the brutality committed against Murat, which we believed necessary to mobilize German public opinion, I could hear nearby on the dais the quiet, pained weeping of Rabiye. During this conference, Rabiye also spoke—simply and eloquently, while holding up a picture of Murat at age eighteen, so that all could understand the human suffering his disappearance inflicted. She explained that she had always thought America was a democracy, so she could not understand how this kind of secrecy and injustice could happen there. Many months later she would tell me that she finally appreciated that Americans were not all bad people, despite what happened to Murat, because of all of the enormous kindness, support, and help she received from Americans concerned about her and Murat's case. Rabiye's perspective reveals what impression foreigners, who never have access to the kindness of ordinary Americans, have of our country and the prison Thomas Friedman aptly suggested represents the "anti Statue of Liberty."*

On the following days, in Berlin, we attended meetings with high-level officials in the Schroeder government, who basically repeated to us what I had heard from the consular official in Washington. The official Berlin line was that because Murat was not technically a German citizen (or, in the revealing words of one German judge who was part of an

---

* Thomas Friedman, "Just Shut it Down," *New York Times*, May 27, 2005, Op-Ed.

audience listening to my depiction of Murat's ordeal, "he is not German!") there was nothing the Foreign Ministry could do on his behalf. Bernhard and I did our best in the press to cast this as a morally bankrupt position that forsook international law and that implicated Germany in the illegality and hypocrisy of Guantanamo. I believe Bernhard's typically eloquent mantra was, "they have imported Guantanamo into German law." The press took great interest in Murat's case; in addition to hundreds of articles in German papers, accounts of his plight appeared repeatedly in the *Washington Post*, the *New York Times*, *Wall Street Journal*, *Boston Globe*, *The New Yorker* magazine, and in many other publications.*

On the last day of this exhausting, but seemingly productive trip, Bernhard and I planned to relax and have a celebratory dinner. That mid-afternoon, however, Rabiye alerted Bernhard that the Turkish media was reporting that Murat had been released and was soon to arrive in the American Air Force base in southern Turkey. Was it true? Who knew? I tried desperately to contact government lawyers, to see if they could tell us anything, but it was Saturday. Also, U.S. government lawyers took the position that detainee lawyers had no right to know in advance of a client's release (this would change after we obtained a court order requiring the government to give us thirty days advance notice of his transfer from Guantanamo, in case the government would try to ship him to a country out of the court's jurisdiction); so, in general, when detainees

---

* For just a few examples, see Carol Leonnig, "Panel Ignored Evidence on Detainee: U.S. Intelligence, German Authorities, Found No Tie to Terrorists," *Washington Post*, March 27, 2005; Carol Leonnig and Dana Priest, "Pentagon Inquiry Is Said to Confirm Muslims' Accounts of Sexual Tactics at Guantanamo," *Washington Post*, February 9, 2005; Shannon Smiley and Craig Whitlock, "Turk Was Abused at Guantanamo, Lawyers Say," *Washington Post*, August 26, 2006; "U.S. Frees Longtime Detainee," *Washington Post*, August 25, 2006; Richard Bernstein, "One Muslim's Odyssey to Guantanamo," *New York Times*, June 5, 2005; Mark Landler and Saoud Mekhennet, "German Detainee Questions His Country's Role," *New York Times*, November 4, 2006; Charlie Savage, "U.S. Orders 38 Freed from Guantanamo," *Boston Globe*, March 30, 2005; Jane Mayer, "The Experiment," *New Yorker*, July 11, 2005; Stacy Sullivan, "Minutes of the Guantanamo Bay Bar Association," *New York Magazine*, June 26, 2006; Jess Bravin, "U.S. Discloses Some Details on Gitmo Captives," *Wall Street Journal*, October 21, 2004.

were released, lawyers only learned about it from the media or family members. It was enough to cause me to cancel my flight home and arrange to fly with Bernhard, Rabiye, and Murat's brothers Ali and Alper the next day to Istanbul to, hopefully, greet Murat when he arrived.

On the flight to Istanbul, the family was ecstatic, exchanging loving glances and hugs in jubilant expectation of this long-awaited moment. They arranged to stay one month in Turkey, to give Murat enough time to get acclimated and to get reacquainted, while we would figure out how to get him home to Germany. Alas, as the evening wore on into morning, their joyful anticipation slowly melted into confused and painful disappointment and finally again into despair: Murat was not coming home. He had never left Guantanamo. This was all an excited Turkish press rumor chasing after itself and fed to a desperate mother who wanted nothing more in the world to believe—and reaffirm—its truth.

It would be another 15 months before the family received word of his return. This time, it was true. In the intervening period, more questions were raised about the German responsibility for Murat's continued detention, in particular regarding the charges—reported by Murat to me and relayed to Bernhard—that Germans had visited Murat in Guantanamo to interrogate him. This certainly undermined the German position that they had no role in his detention and were unable to even approach the Americans to discuss his release. Soon after this revelation, and other urgent questions about Germany's role in the American support of the war on terror, the new German Chancellor, Angela Merkel, announced publicly in Germany that she would broach the issue of the repatriation of Murat in an upcoming meeting with President Bush. Perhaps the Bush Administration was more willing now to reduce the population of the increasingly criticized prison camp, or perhaps it needed to do the new, conservative Chancellor Merkel a diplomatic favor; in any event, the Bush Administration finally agreed to negotiate for Murat's release. The negotiations took over eight months, apparently because the American side was insisting on conditions to which the German government, happily, would not accede—such as confiscation of

Murat's passport, preventative detention, and other surveillance meas-
ures presumably prohibited by German law.

By December 2005 Bernhard and I felt confident that his release
would occur. I was eager to report these developments to Murat in person, but my trips were repeatedly delayed. When I attempted to visit
with him in January 2006, the military told me on two consecutive days
that Murat "refuses his attorney visit." I was struck by the earnestness
with which the commander delivered this message; lawyers had long
joked that the only right the military guards respect is the detainees'
right to refuse counsel.

Nevertheless, it seemed incomprehensible that Murat would refuse
to see me; we had such a good relationship; he trusted me; I always
brought him food. While on the island, I wrote Murat notes enticing him
with important news, which the military promised to deliver for me in
person that day so that he might reconsider his decision. Apparently,
those didn't work either; the military repeated that he refused to see me.
I was still immensely confused and alarmed. It had been a long time since
I had seen him; perhaps he had, like so many other detainees, lost hope
or developed an intense resentment towards this endless, unproductive
legal process. Or, perhaps he had simply lost his wits. That same day,
there was a huge rally for Murat in Bremen, where Bernhard was to
announce that I was visiting Murat that same day, and that he was still in
good spirits. How dreadfully ironic.

When I returned home, dejected and concerned, I immediately
scheduled another visit. I was not going to give up after all this time. If he
didn't want to see me, if he had lost faith in me or this process, he'd have
to tell me in person; he owed me at least that much. In May, I returned to
Guantanamo. When I entered the meeting room, he was sitting there as
usual, apparently happy to see me. I wanted to handle this potentially
awkward moment delicately.

"Murat, why did you refuse my visit in January?"

Murat smiled broadly, as if to say, "Don't you know better by now
than to believe what they tell you?" As it turned out, the military had

never told him in January, as they had represented, that he had a lawyer visit. And, what about the handwritten notes I asked to be delivered to him on those days? He received them in February—three weeks after I left—along with a letter I had sent through the legal mail system, after it was obviously too late to have any effect.

There was nothing really to do about this—it was one of dozens of inconveniences and obstacles habeas counsel dealt with, and there was no point obsessing over it. Murat was seemingly healthy, in reasonably good spirits, and there was something he could look forward to. Mindful of the previous disastrous false alarm, I was somewhat reluctant to get his hopes up. Nevertheless, I explained that there was very good reason to believe he'd be released within a few months. He was cautious, trying to conceal any emotions. Perhaps he didn't want to be disappointed. By the second day of that visit however, we broached this possibility, discussing what he would want to eat first ("have my father prepare a lamb"), what he would buy (a motorcycle; he'd take me on the Autobahn at 150 kph), and the immense amounts of attention he'd receive upon his return. He laughed at my suggestion that the press would be everywhere, including in the trees and under cars, to get a picture of him, as if he were a prized Hollywood celebrity. "I will be like Tom Cruise?" he joked.

In August 2006, German officials told Berhnard and me the date that Murat would likely be released, which gave me enough time to fly to Germany for the occasion. On August 24, 2006, Bernhard and I met the whole Kurnaz family at a gas station outside of Bremen for the six-hour drive south toward Ramstein Air Force base, where we were told he would be arriving in the early evening. The day was full of intrigue—secret meetings with German officials to find out the location of the meeting place for the Kurnaz family reunion—constant, intrusive calls from German and American reporters demanding confirmation of a spreading rumor of his release, and almost overwhelming anxiety. While we awaited Murat's arrival in a Red Cross senior citizens' facility, we saw through the window a huge C-17 military plane descending from the sky. It was Murat.

From the window, Bernhard saw Murat enter the building along with the affable German foreign ministry officials who earlier told us where the dropoff and reunion would be. Rabiye, Murat's father, Ali, Alper, Bernhard, and I all assembled in the hallway on the fourth floor to greet Murat. Despite all my prior descriptions, Bernhard still seemed stunned when he caught a quick glimpse of Murat's beard through the window. Rabiye stood in front of the creaky elevator doors; her anticipation built to an almost unbearable level as the elevator repeatedly started and stopped, huffed and creaked. Finally when the doors opened, Rabiye latched onto her son as if he might be taken away from her again at any moment; with Murat in her arms, she wept helplessly for a long time.

In the incredible excitement of that very long day, including a 3 AM rush into the Kurnaz home past a swarm of waiting journalists, I remember one thing more clearly than any other. During the many hours that Murat and I had spent together in Guantanamo, his ankle had always been chained to the floor. That day, for the first time, I saw Murat walk.

———————

I am now relieved and gratified that Murat has claimed back much of his prior life—at least his family, his friends, and his hobbies. Murat's written account of his horrible odyssey, however, is, in my mind, the most powerful and enduring reclamation of his dignity. Milan Kundera, the absurdist critic of soviet totalitarianism wrote that "the struggle of man against power is the struggle of memory against forgetting."* Because Kundera believed that the great tool of undemocratic regimes is to use their power to alter or reconstruct reality, he thought it essential that artists, journalists, and dissidents make a record of their memory as a form of resistance and of truth. Murat's memoir, along with other accounts of U.S. government actions in Guantanamo—which would

———————

* Milan Kundera, *The Book of Laughter and Forgetting* (New York: HarperPerennial, 1999).

otherwise remain secret or deeply distorted—provide vital testimony to a profound injustice; this book represents one small but important strike against unchecked power.

Baher Azmy is a professor of law at Seton Hall Law School in Newark, New Jersey, where he teaches constitutional law and litigates in the area of civil rights. He remains involved in the litigation related to the Guantanamo Bay detentions. He lives in New York City with his wife Margo, and their two-year-old daughter, Laila.